# The Mystery
## Which Has Been Hidden

## By Edward Kurath

# *The Mystery Which Has Been Hidden*

All rights reserved. No part of this book may be reproduced or transmitted in any form or by any means, electronic or mechanical, including photocopying, recording or by any information storage and retrieval system, without written permission from the author, except for the inclusion of brief quotations.

Copyright © 2016 by Edward Kurath
Published by: Divinely Designed
24326 Winder Place, Golden, Colorado 80403
**www.divinelydesigned.com**

ISBN 978-9764551-6-21

First printing 2016

Printed in the United States of America

Copyright Permission:
All scripture quotations, unless otherwise indicated, are taken from the New King James Version ® Copyright © 1982 by Thomas Nelson, Inc. Used by permission. All rights reserved.

# Table of Contents

# Introduction

I pray that what I have written here will be a great blessing to you. It reveals a great mystery that had been hidden until the coming of Jesus Christ.

> *The mystery which has been hidden from ages and from generations, but now has been revealed to His saints* (Colossians 1:26).

Truly, His advent here is the greatest event in the history of mankind. And yet the full potency of what He provided has continued to be a great mystery to many Christians.

This book is written to those who have made Jesus Christ their Lord. Those who have not done so will not find any of this to be useful, because it does not apply to them (of course, you may become a Christian by making Jesus Christ your Lord. See page 11 for a prayer).

So let's pull back the curtain and see the great truth that has been so hidden, so mysterious.

# Chapter 1

## You Own A Buried Treasure

### The Good News

There is a treasure of which you are likely unaware. It is only available to those who belong to Jesus. It is yours. To possess it, you just need to accept it.

If you truly grasped the amazing blessing of the treasure, you would be willing to give up everything else you have in order to possess it. That is what Jesus was talking about in Matthew:

> *"Again, the kingdom of heaven is like treasure hidden in a field, which a man found and hid; and for joy over it he goes and sells all that he has and buys that field" (Matthew 11:44).*

> *"who, when he had found one pearl of great price, went and sold all that he had and bought it" (Matthew 11:46).*

What is Jesus talking about, that would be that valuable, that would be more valuable than anything else you could possess? Is there such a "pearl" that you can find and possess?

Here "treasure" and "pearl of great price" are metaphors for the great gift of salvation that Jesus has made available to mankind.

In fact, this "pearl" is of such value that Jesus was willing to be sacrificed to come down from heaven, suffer, die, and rise again to give it to us. This was indeed a great sacrifice He made, and He suffered greatly to provide for us.

*For scarcely for a righteous man will one die; yet perhaps for a good man someone would even dare to die. But God demonstrates His own love toward us, in that while we were still sinners, Christ died for us. Much more then, having now been justified by His blood, we shall be saved from wrath through Him. For if when we were enemies we were reconciled to God through the death of His Son, much more, having been reconciled, we shall be saved by His life* (Romans 5:7-10).

Note that here there is both a past and a future benefit inferred: *having been justified* (past), *we shall be saved* (future). Through this amazing treasure, Jesus did provide us with life after death, but He also provided what we need to be victorious over sin in this life.

There is nothing to compare with this salvation, and yet it is a free gift that is ours for the taking.

This great gift that Jesus provided for us has **two aspects**.

1. There is a **one-time event** that occurs when we give our life to Jesus. In that one act we become children of God. This radically changes our relationship to God, and gives Him the right to treat us as His children.

2.

3. We have to act in order to bring this about: *Confess with your mouth the Lord Jesus, and believe in your heart that God raised Him from the dead* **(Romans 10:9).**

We are all familiar with this aspect, and are undoubtedly greatly thankful for it. It is a miraculous provision only available through the sacrifice of our Savior. Through it, when we leave this earth we will live forever in the presence of God. It also provides special privileges that we now have as sons of God.

> *To redeem those who were under the law, that we might receive the adoption as sons. And because you are sons, God has sent forth the Spirit of His Son into your hearts, crying out, "Abba, Father!" Therefore you are no longer a slave but a son, and if a son, then an heir of God through Christ* (Galatians 4:5-7).

This new reality also gives God permission to work in our lives for our welfare. For instance:

> *Furthermore, we have had earthly fathers to discipline us, and we respected them; shall we not much rather be subject to the Father of spirits, and live? For they disciplined us for a short time as seemed best to them, but He disciplines us for our good, that we may share His holiness.* (Hebrews 12:9-10 NAS).

**By accepting Jesus as our Lord, reality has changed for us!**

## What then?

Once we have "been saved" (this one-time event), is it up to us to try hard to be a good Christian, including doing our best to obey God's commandments?

## NO. A thousand times no!

If that were the case, from a daily living standpoint, Christianity would be no different than the rest of the world's religions. There the believers have certain things they need to do in order to be in the good graces of their god.

Christianity is very different than that. Jesus Christ provided a way for the children of God to live sinless lives!

> *"For this is the covenant that I will make with the house of Israel after those days, says the Lord: I will put My laws in their minds and write them on their hearts; and I will be their God, and they shall be My people"* . . . *In that He says, "A new covenant,", He has made the first obsolete* (Hebrews 8:10, 13).

To make this happen, there is a second aspect to this miraculous treasure that Jesus provided for us after we have become children of God:

**The second aspect is:**

**2. There is then a <u>lifelong process</u> whereby we are literally transformed into the image of Jesus. This is a process whereby step-by-step He removes our areas of sin and inhabits those areas. As this occurs, we will step-by-step act like Jesus because of our new Christ-like nature there. In the Bible this process frequently is referred to as "sanctification."**

**We also have to act in order to bring this about: *"Forgive and you will be forgiven:]"* (Luke 6:37).**

This second aspect of the treasure is just as miraculous and effective as the first. What is especially amazing about this second aspect is that it is effectual for us during our lifetime here on earth. We really need that! Unfortunately, most Christians are much less aware of this provision than the first one. By this second aspect, Jesus made provision to take away our sins, [1] and in this process give us Jesus' character, <u>during our lifetime.</u>

The New Testament puts a great deal of emphasis on this second aspect. [2] This provision for us in this lifetime produces good things that we can't produce on our own, such as:

## <u>Liberty</u> from the bondage of sin:

> *"The Spirit of the Lord is upon Me, because He has anointed Me to preach the gospel to the poor; He has sent Me to heal the brokenhearted, to proclaim liberty to the captives and recovery of sight to the blind, to set at liberty those who are oppressed"* (Luke 4:18).

Also see Galatians 2:4, which addresses the enemy's early attempt to steal the liberty we have in Christ:

> *And this occurred because of false brethren secretly brought in (who came in by stealth to spy out our liberty which we have in Christ Jesus, that they might bring us into bondage).*

---

[1] Sin is doing anything that will set the spiritual realm to working against you. That is why God tells you what is good to do and what is bad to do. When He tells you what not to do, He is saying: "My child, please don't do this, because you will suffer if you do it." See Chapter 3 for more details about this.

[2] In the Epistles of the New Testament, the first aspect is spoken of 19 times, while the second aspect is mentioned 184 times. Obviously, the writers considered the second aspect to be of great importance to the Christians to whom they were writing. See Appendix B for details.

## Peace in our hearts:

> *"Peace I leave with you. My peace I give to you, not as the world gives do I give to you. Let not your heart be troubled, neither let it be afraid"* (John 14:27).

> *And the peace of God, which surpasses all understanding, will guard your hearts and minds through Christ Jesus* (Philippians 4:7).

Also see John 14:27, John 16:33, Acts 10:36, 2 Corinthians 1:2, Philippians 4:7; Colossians 1:2.

## Rest from striving:

> *"Come to Me, all you who labor and are heavy laden, and I will give you rest. Take My yoke upon you and learn from Me, for I am gentle and lowly in heart, and you will find rest for your souls. For My yoke is easy and My burden is light"* (Matthew 11:28-30).

## Freedom:

> *"Therefore if the Son makes you free, you shall be free indeed"* (John 8:36).

These are all things we can't produce ourselves. They are gifts from God through Jesus Christ. In saying these things, God is not taunting us with the impossibility of obtaining these things. They must therefore be possible and available to us through the sacrifice of Jesus, and they are. If they are not occurring in your life, the problem undoubtedly is that you haven't been taught HOW these things can be yours through Christ Jesus.

# These Are Free Gifts

It is almost beyond our ability to comprehend the magnitude of these aspects of salvation. And to add to their amazing reality, these aspects are free gifts. All we have to do is to appropriate them. But we do have to understand how to do this. As a Christian, you already possess the first gift - eternal life. Now you need to learn how to possess the second gift – being freed from your sins and being transformed into the image of Jesus as a result.

## My purpose here is to teach you how to appropriate this second free gift that is yours for the taking!

### If You Are Not a Christian

If you are not a Christian, and you would like to inherit these two blessed gifts, you can very simply accept Him as Lord. The Bible says:

> *That if you confess with your mouth the Lord Jesus and believe in your heart that God has raised Him from the dead, you will be saved* (Romans 10:9).

It is very simple. Just say something like: "Jesus, I believe that You are the Christ, the Savior, and that God raised you from the dead. I ask You to become the Lord of my life. I surrender myself to You."[3]

And right then He will accept you into the family of God!

---

[3] A more extensive prayer that explains more completely your change in status might be: "Dear Father God in heaven, I come to you in the name of Jesus. I acknowledge to You that I am a sinner, and I am sorry for my sins and the life that I have lived; I need your forgiveness. I believe that your only begotten Son Jesus Christ shed His precious blood on the cross at Calvary and died for my sins, and I am now willing to turn from my sin. You said in Your Holy Word, Romans 10:9 that if we confess the Lord our God and believe in our hearts that God raised Jesus from the dead, we shall be saved. Right now I confess Jesus as the Lord of my life. With my heart, I believe that God raised Jesus from the dead. This very moment I accept Jesus Christ as my own personal Savior and according to His Word, right now I am saved."

# Chapter 2

## What Is This "Pearl Of Great Price"?

This gift of salvation is referred to as a mystery that men have sought for all of time.

> . . . *The mystery which has been hidden from ages and from generations, but now has been revealed to His saints. To them God willed to make known what are the riches of the glory of this mystery among the Gentiles: which is Christ in you, the hope of glory* (Colossians 1:25-27, underlining is mine).

Paul is here writing to Christians, so he must be referring to the second great gift of sanctification as being the mystery, which is God's will: "which is Christ in you."

> *Now to Him who is able to establish you according to my gospel and the preaching of Jesus Christ, according to the revelation of the mystery kept secret since the world began* (Romans 16:25).

It is true that man has always been seeking a cure for sin. They knew they did bad things, and created all sorts of rituals designed to keep them from suffering the consequences of their sin. But they found no cure.

But we now finally have the cure for sin through Jesus Christ. I would like to help you to understand this mystery, so that the gift can be effectual in your life.

Because this is a mystery, it can be hard to grasp conceptually. Therefore I am going to give you a concrete example from my own life that graphically shows the problem we have because of our Adamic nature, and the miraculous rescue available through the blood sacrifice of Jesus Christ.

I am a jogger, and for years I lived on the side of a mountain. In the winter it is icy, and I can't run here; because I might fall and break something. Therefore I drive 4 miles to town. There is a street that is about 1 1/2 miles out and 1 1/2 miles back that is plowed and sanded and does not have much traffic. That is my running track in the winter.

One day a few years ago I was almost at the far end of the run when two mid-sized dogs ran out after me. I have learned that you don't run from dogs, so I turned on them and I shouted,

"Hey, you get back there."

They skidded to a stop. The owner was a woman who was standing on the sidewalk. She said,

"Hey, don't talk to my dogs like that."

I said, "Lady, you have to be kidding me. We are in town, there is a leash law here. Your dogs shouldn't be here in the street."

She called her dogs and went inside.

As I continued my run, I was very upset.

I thought, "This is the only convenient place I have to run, and I'm not going to let them spoil that. What will I do about it? I know what. I have a foot long steel bar in my garage. I'll carry that. Then when they come out, I'll take care of them."

Then I thought again. It wasn't really the dogs' fault, and I'd probably get in trouble if I hurt them. Then what can I do instead?

"I know what I'll do," I thought. "I'll carry my cell phone. Then when they come out after me, I'll grab one of them by the collar and call the dog warden. Then she'll get a ticket, and that should fix her."

I finished my run, drove home, showered and dressed, and went to my office. As I sat down, I was still chewing over this situation. As I grumbled over it, I got the distinct impression that the Lord was tapping me on the shoulder. I knew what He wanted: He wanted me to forgive the woman. I didn't want to forgive her, and argued with the Lord.

"But she was so thoughtless.  She had no right to let her dogs loose, etc, etc, etc."

Eventually I realized I was going to lose the argument.  I reluctantly agreed to forgive her, though I still didn't want to.  I was fully convinced I was right, and she was wrong.

Initially as I prayed it was pretty mechanical and wooden.  However, as I prayed, gradually I calmed down; and the forgiveness became more real.  I forgave her, asked the Lord to forgive me for judging her.  I asked Him to take out the bitter root I had just planted, to cleanse that place, and to fill it with His Holy Spirit.

As I prayed, I began to recognize that she had a permanent scowl on her face.  It also occurred to me that a healthy person would have said something like,

"I'm sorry, sir.  Are you alright?  Did my dogs scare you?"

I realized that she seemed to be a wounded and unhappy person.  I felt compassion for her, and I began to pray for her.  I suspected that she might not know the Lord, and I began to pray for her salvation.

Suddenly it was as though I was struck by lightning.  The change in my mindset was stark.  I realized that I was now seeing her the way the Lord sees her.  I wasn't praying for her salvation because it was the "Christian thing to do."  I was praying for her because I saw her pain and neediness.

**I realized that a miracle had occurred in me!**

Before I prayed, I was a bit crazy.  I was on the throne, she was wrong, and I was sure I was right.  I was in the mind of the "flesh." [4]  Bad fruit (my plans to make her pay) was coming from that bitter root.

> **I realized that a miracle had occurred!**

---

[4]  Romans 8:6-7 describes how this mindset works: *For to be carnally minded is death, but to be spiritually minded is life and peace.  Because the carnal mind is enmity against God; for it is not subject to the law of God, nor indeed can be.*

After I prayed, I saw her neediness and wounding. I was now seeing her as Christ saw her. I now had the mind of Christ. Jesus was now in me where the bitter root had previously been planted, and that new good root was producing good fruit (my compassion for her). I wasn't trying to see her with eyes of compassion. I simply did.

I included this experience of mine, because it is so typical of our daily struggle with sin.

I would like to point out some important aspects of this common event of mine.

1. This was an ordinary, common event. It was not a huge, traumatic, life changing event. It was the sort of thing that we all experience many times a day.
2. When we feel transgressed, we always react with bitterness, judgment, and blame.
3. After I judged the woman, I was fully convinced that she was wrong, I was right, and I was going to find a way to make her pay.
4. My anger was my friend who was telling me that I had judged.
5. At first, I did not want to forgive the woman. I was totally opposed to doing so, and argued with the Lord about it. I was being dominated by the mindset of the "flesh." This was the point where I had to exercise my will power: not to change how I saw her, but to decide to forgive.
6. As I prayed, to start with it was reluctantly. But I stuck with it, and it became heartfelt.
7. As I forgave and was forgiven, and asked the Lord to remove my bitter root and to come into that place and fill it with His Spirit, He did so.
8. A complete reversal of my viewpoint occurred when He filled me. I began to see the woman through His eyes, and was fully convinced of this new perspective.

9. This change in perspective <u>was a miracle</u>. The change was not based on logic or rationalization on my part. It was not a conscious decision. In fact, I was surprised at my change in attitude. It was imparted to me by Jesus inside me in response to my prayer.

When we forgive and Jesus forgives us, <u>a miracle occurs</u>. It is not something we can accomplish on our own. We can repress our anger, or try to be nice; but we can't change what is inside us. Only the blood of Jesus can accomplish that change. And He does it! This

> **This pattern of consistently forgiving and being forgiven by Jesus is meant to be the normal Christian life!**

pattern is meant to be the normal Christian life!

Our problem is sin. The cure is the sacrifice of Jesus (the second aspect of the miraculous treasure He has provided for us).

In this example, I perceived that a person had transgressed against me, and I judged her. That is sin. So I forgave her, and the Lord forgave me for having judged her, and He came into that bitter place in me, washed it clean, and inhabited that place. Now I was indeed just like Jesus in that area of my life. I had been sanctified.

The scripture is clear, that judging is a sin that will cause us to suffer.

> *Judge not, that you be not judged. For with what judgment you judge, you will be judged; and with the measure you use, it will be measured back to you"* (Mathew 7:1-2).

But forgiving will take away our sin and the consequences of our judging.

*"Judge not, and you shall not be judged. Condemn not, and you shall not be condemned. Forgive, and you will be forgiven"* (Luke 6:37).

## Our Problem

Our problem is that **we do judge**. It is done spontaneously and subconsciously, out of our Adamic nature. It has happened before we know it. There is no way to avoid doing it. This tendency will be with us as long as we walk this earth. Therefore, since we can't stop from doing it, what we need to do is to forgive <u>every time</u> it happens.

Here Luke 6:37 makes it clear that we need to forgive in order to be forgiven.

*"And forgive us our sins, for we also forgive everyone who is indebted to us"* (Luke 11:4).

When we judge, we are convinced that the other person owes us a debt. When we forgive, we "write off" that debt, and then the other person owes us nothing. [5]

This is made clear in what we call the Lord's Prayer:

*"Our Father in heaven, hallowed be Your name. Your kingdom come, Your will be done on earth as it is in heaven. Give us this day our daily bread, and <u>forgive us our debts, as we forgive our debtors</u>, and do not lead us into temptation, but deliver us from the evil one. For Yours is the kingdom and the power and the glory forever. Amen."* (Matthew 6:12, underlining is mine).

---

[5] The Greek word usually translated as "forgive" is *aphiemi* (Strong's 863). It means generally "to send forth or away, let go from oneself. . . Metaphorically, to let go from obligation toward oneself, to remit, e.g., a debt, offense" (Zodhiates P. 299).

We judge a lot, so we need to forgive a lot.

> *Then Peter came to Him and said, "Lord, how often shall my brother sin against me, and I forgive him? Up to seven times?" Jesus said to him, "I do not say to you up to seven time4s, but up to seventy times seven"* (Matthew 18:21-22).

There are some important things to note here:
- First of all, Peter will judge his brother <u>every time</u> he transgressed against him. How do we know this? Peter would not have to forgive his brother if he hadn't judged him.
- Second, it will happen a lot.
- Third, the Lord will forgive Peter every time he judges his brother, no matter how often it happens. There is no quota beyond which the Lord will no longer forgive Peter, as long as he first forgives. Why does Peter judge his brother every time he sins against him? He does this because he is of Adam's race and has this propensity to sin by judging others. It happens lots of times. See Chapter 8 for more about this trait.

<u>We are just like Peter</u>. God knows our fallen nature, and so He sent Jesus to provide a way to clean up the messes we continuously make. There is no evidence in scripture that we will ever stop sinning as long as we walk this earth. Therefore, we all need the Savior many times a day as long as we live.

All of this may seem so familiar to you that you may say "so what?" If this is your thought, I would say that you do not grasp the magnitude of this gift of forgiveness of our sins. <u>This is the "pearl of great price"</u> for which we would be

> **Forgiveness for our sins is the "pearl of great price."**

willing to give up everything else in our lives – if we understood it's value. This was not available to mankind until Jesus died to provide it.

Why do we neglect this wonderful gift?  Typically, it may be because of several factors:

- We don't realize that judging is sin.
- We don't realize it when we have just judged.
- We don't realize how frequently we judge.
- We don't realize that we will experience a negative consequence for every time we judge and don't forgive.
- It is hard for us to admit we are wrong.
- Above all, we haven't been taught about this.  It has not been emphasized in most churches, so we are not aware of the central importance of this dynamic of judging and forgiving.

If you sin and do not repent, you will have bad things happen to you. Paul refers to this consequence as "death."

> *"For the wages of sin is death, but the gift of God is eternal life in Christ Jesus our Lord"* (Romans 6:23)

Without the forgiveness by Jesus, nobody ever escapes the deadly consequences of sin.  There are no exceptions to this, which is why we need the Savior – to save us from our sins.

Consequently, being unaware of this treasure available to you not only causes you to miss out on the miraculous blessing of the blood of Jesus (the forgiveness of your sins, daily), but it also causes you to reap the consequences of your sins.  You will suffer.  God doesn't want that to happen to you, which is why He sent Jesus.

## It Gets Worse

Unfortunately, for a Christian to neglect the forgiveness of their sins through Jesus Christ, there is more bad stuff coming down the road than the just consequence for the un-repented sin. When we neglect this gift He freely gave us, we are treating it as though it is unimportant and irrelevant to our life. This may not be our intention, but nevertheless it is a fact.

> *For this reason we must pay much closer attention to what we have heard, lest we drift away from it. For if the word spoken through angels proved unalterable, and <u>every transgression</u> and disobedience received a <u>just recompense</u>, how shall we escape <u>if we neglect so great a salvation</u>? After it was at the first spoken through the Lord, it was confirmed to us by those who heard* (Hebrews 2:1-3, NAS. Underlining is mine).

The book of Hebrews was written to Christians, so the readers had already been "saved" – the one-time event. So therefore the "great a salvation" here referred to must be referring to the ongoing gift of sanctification.

Note the word "neglect." It is not saying "reject." It is not that the readers had rejected Jesus provision, but that they had begun to ignore it. The Greek word here translated as "neglect" is *ameleo* (Strong's #272). It means "Not to care for, to neglect" (Zodhiates p. 132). So it does not refer to hostility or active rejection of Jesus and His provision for us, but to forgetting about it, to counting it as unimportant.

**Do you continuously apply the blood to all your sins?**

Here there is not a detailed description of what "just recompense" means, but we can assume that it is something very negative.

The writer then goes on to further emphasize how bad it is to neglect your sanctification, and the consequences of neglecting it, and thus how severe is the "recompense":

> *Anyone who did set a law of Moses <u>as nothing</u>, apart from mercies, by two or three witnesses, does die, of how much sorer punishment shall he be counted worthy <u>who did trample on the Son of God, and did count the blood of the covenant a **common thing,**</u> in which he was sanctified, and did despite to the Spirit of the grace? For we have known Him who is saying, "Vengeance [js] Mine, I will recompense, says the Lord:"* and again, *"The Lord shall judge His people;" – fearful [is] the falling into the hands of a living God* (Hebrews 10: 28-31, Young's Literal Translation, underline and bold is mine).

The word here translated as "common" is Greek *koinos* (Strong's 2839). In this verse several bibles translate this as "unholy." However, in context, "common" fits much better. In the previous verse 28, it is not saying that "anyone" is calling the law of Moses as "unholy", but as <u>nothing important</u>. Thus in verse 29 that meaning carries through. In this context, *koinos* means "to lie common or open to all, common or belonging to several or of which several are partakers (Acts 2:44; 4:32; Titus 1:4; Jude 1:3 . . . unconsecrated and therefore having no atoning efficacy) such as were common to other nations but were avoided by the Jews as polluted and unclean (Mark 7:2)" (Zodhiates p. 872). The blood of Jesus (His provision to wash away our sin) <u>is not "common,"</u> meaning open to every human, but is a unique, special gift only available to the children of God.

This scripture is therefore saying that <u>neglecting to apply</u> the blood of Jesus to your sins is essentially trampling on the Son of God, and will result in "sorer punishment" than was experienced by those of old who ignored the law of Moses (there the punishment was death!). <u>Neglecting to apply the blood of Jesus is a serious issue!</u>

Sanctification by the blood of Jesus is a special, miraculous provision only available to those who have made Him their Lord. It is not a "common thing" to be treated as nothing.

> **If you fail to routinely apply the blood of Jesus to your sins, you trample on the Son of God!**

If you neglect your sanctification, Hebrews 10:29 above says you are treating it as unimportant, and **you trample on the Son of God!** Very strong language. And there is a very negative consequence for doing this. To repeat part of the prior scripture:

> *For we know Him who said, "Vengeance is Mine, I will repay," says the Lord. And again, "The Lord will judge His people." It is a fearful thing to fall into the hands of the living God* (Hebrews 10:30-31).

This elaborates on "much worse punishment" mentioned in verse 29. It is clear that this neglect is a sin, and it is not simply passed over or ignored because you don't think it is important, or don't know the consequences for neglecting it.

I'll bet you didn't know this, and I would also bet that you would never want to be insulting the Lord. But do you neglect His salvation by **not continuously applying** the blood of Jesus to your sins [6] by forgiving and being forgiven? If you do neglect it, you are in a bad place!

---

[6] By far the most destructive sin is judging. When we do judge (which we do very frequently), we are taking the Lord's place. He is the only one Who has the right to judge. See Chapter 5 for more detail on judging, and Chapter 6 on forgiving.

Because of the consequences written in these scriptures, it would be wise to consider their message. It is logical that this message would be in the book of Hebrews, because the importance of the blood sacrifice of Jesus is the primary focus of that whole book. Before Jesus came, we were all stuck in our sins. His sacrifice is the only cure for our frequent sins. It is a miracle He came to give us, because He loves us.

## Our sanctification is a treasure that is ours for the taking!

## Where To Go From Here?

If you would like to appropriate this treasure of your sanctification through Jesus Christ, then I would like to give you some additional information so that you can indeed claim the blessings that are there for the taking.

For you to accomplish this it will be helpful for me to give you more background information, so that you not only know what to do, but why. The scriptures are rich in teachings about this journey. In Appendix B I have listed most of the passages in the Epistles that refer to the ongoing process of sanctification. Now I would like to pull this all together so that you will be equipped to move forward with the Lord.

Some more good news is that as you seek to walk in the Lord's ways, He will actively guide you on your journey. You are not in this alone. As you read through the following chapters, it will become clearer to you how He will guide you. God loves you, and He sent His Son to die for you to provide for you this great treasure of freedom from sin.

The next chapter will describe the spiritual realm, and why our will power is unable to control spiritual events. It will then become clearer why we can't save ourselves, and why we need the Savior!

# Chapter 3

# The Power of the Spirit Realm
## *God's Laws At Work*

> *For what I am doing, I do not understand. For what I will to do, that I do not practice; but what I hate, that I do* **(Romans 7:15).**

These words haunt many of us. This is the common experience of all those who are trying to please the Lord, who want to walk in His ways.

God knows that you continually fail, and He wants it to be different. He wants so much to set you free from this bondage that He sent Jesus to make it possible.

There is a clear and profound reason why we are all stuck doing what we don't want to do, and I will now go on to explain why.

## The Reality God Created

When God created the universe, He created it to operate in an orderly way in accordance with unchangeable laws. There are three aspects, or realms, to the reality we experience:

1. **The physical**
2. **The spiritual**
3. **The psychological** [7]

---

[7] Some would call this the realm of the "soul." However, I have avoided using the word "soul" because it is loaded with meaning to many Christians. It is usually perceived as referring to something negative or sinful. But in the Bible "soul" has many meanings, some referring to something sinful, but often not. What I am referring to here is not "bad," but rather is simply an aspect of life which is based upon our own strengths and abilities and natural tendencies. As with the physical world, in and of itself, the psychological realm carries no moral significance. It just exists.

## The Physical Realm

We can all see the orderliness of the physical realm. The physical laws, such as those of physics, chemistry, and mathematics, are unchangeable. We may not fully understand them, and we may misapply them, but they still operate. Since the New York Trade Center Towers fell in the terrorist attack, there are studies going on to understand what was wrong with their design that allowed them to fall. These studies are being done in order to see if we can learn something that will prevent such collapses in buildings of the future. We can learn how to prevent it because the laws of physics are constant. There are no exceptions. Nobody thinks the Towers fell because something went wrong with the laws of physics.

If I were to go onto the roof of my house, convinced that I can fly, flap my arms really hard and step off the roof, I would make a discovery. I would then discover myself lying on the ground with a broken leg. It wouldn't matter whether I knew about the law of gravity or not. It wouldn't matter if I understood it, or whether I agreed with it, or whether I believed in it. It wouldn't matter how much faith I had that gravity didn't apply to me. My broken leg wouldn't mean God was angry with me. I didn't break God's law, all I did was demonstrate it. The law of gravity is constant. There are no exceptions.

## The Spiritual Realm

The spiritual realm (another aspect of reality) is just as orderly as is the physical realm, and it always operates according to unchangeable laws and principles. God told us about these laws in the Bible. His commandments are simply a description of how the spiritual realm operates. When He said not to lie, He was saying, "Please don't lie; because if you do, something bad will happen to you." It is the same as God saying, "Please don't step off the roof, because something bad will happen if you do." In the physical realm, nobody ever defied the law of gravity. The spiritual realm is just as sure, and so nobody ever gets away with anything. There is always a consequence. The law of God always operates. [8] Disobeying God's warning is what we call sin. When we sin, we will <u>always</u> reap harmful consequences. The consequences are often less immediate and less easy to connect to our specific misdeed than when we are reaping from physical laws, but they are just as sure.

## The Psychological Realm

The third aspect of reality is the psychological realm. The psychological realm operates in accordance with our own powers and abilities. Habit patterns, our intellect, and our own willpower are aspects of the psychological realm. Our willpower has been given to us as a tool to manage this psychological realm, and it has authority there. If I have a habit of brushing my teeth without flossing, and I decide to start flossing, I can generally

> **Disobeying God's warning is what we call "sin."**

succeed in doing so. I may forget from time to time, but eventually the new habit pattern will be established. I experience victory.

## We Have Made A Huge Mistake

But we have made a huge mistake, because we have believed that our willpower also has authority in the spiritual realm. However, our willpower <u>only</u> has authority in the psychological realm. We cannot overcome or defy the physical laws or spiritual laws with our willpower.

Our willpower is impotent in defying the laws of the physical realm, and it was never given to us for this purpose. We cannot fly by flapping our arms. We cannot lift a 500 pound weight. We discover that no matter how much we want to lift it, we can't. We can will it, but we cannot perform it.

---

[8] What I am referring to as "God's laws" are the true ways that God set up the spiritual realm to operate. Man's additions do not have the same power. We may or may not accurately understand God's laws; but since they are true, they operate whether or not we know them or understand them.

What is perhaps harder to understand is that our willpower is as impotent in the spiritual realm as it is in the physical realm. It was never given to us for the purpose of managing the spiritual realm. We discover this impotence when we try to do a spiritually impossible task, like obeying the laws of God. We discover that no matter how hard we want to do the good that we ought to, we cannot. We can "will" it, but we cannot perform it. *O wretched man that I am* (Romans 7:24). Our failure to do the good

> **When we try to use our willpower to control the physical or spiritual realms, we fail.**

that we want to do is not due to a lack of willpower, it is due to our misunderstanding about reality. We are under the illusion that we ought to be able to "will" it and thus do it.

To imagine the relative power of our willpower and the operation of God's laws (the spiritual realm), picture an ant standing on a highway. A huge truck is coming his way at full speed, and the ant thinks he can stop the truck by standing up and blocking its movement with his body.

STOP! ------

The ant's degree of failure is at the same level as our failure to stop the operation of God's laws with our own willpower!  Yet we have been under the delusion that we can do so.  And much worse, we think that God has <u>expected</u> us to be able to do so!

Unfortunately, we have often been led into striving by teachings that imply that we are supposed to be able to live up to the higher standards, as delineated in the Sermon on the Mount in Matthew, Chapter 5.  However, this is not what Jesus is telling us to do.

> **Jesus did <u>not</u> say that you should "act" like Him, but that you should "be" like Him.**

Rather, He is telling us that we cannot possibly do it with our own willpower.

> *"For I say to you, that unless your righteousness exceeds the righteousness of the scribes and Pharisees, you will by no means enter the kingdom of heaven"* (Matthew 5:20).

What was the righteousness of the scribes and Pharisees?  It was their willpower!  And we need a righteousness that exceeds willpower.  Jesus goes on to say that the only way we can truly keep the laws of God is to be changed into His image:

> *"Therefore you shall **be** perfect, just as your Father in heaven is perfect"* (Matthew 5:48 I added the bold).

Jesus did <u>not</u> say, "You shall <u>behave</u> perfectly," but rather He said, "You shall be perfect" (be like Me).  We will have a new existence, a new nature.  We will <u>be</u> like Him!  "Being" like Jesus leads to, and results in, "behavior" like Jesus.

# The Illusion Of Our Willpower

One of the great tragedies in our Western culture is the elevation of our willpower and our intellect to the throne of our life. We think that the only things we can trust are these two faculties. The heart, and anything that we cannot consciously understand or control (such as our emotions) are seen as untrustworthy, or even perhaps as bad. We are stuck in this delusion. Our trust is so firmly entrenched in our willpower and intellect that whenever we are in need, without thinking we automatically rely on our willpower and intellect.

The bumper sticker that says "Just Say No" is a perfect example of this. If people who were hooked on drugs could "Just Say No," many would. Many try - and fail, over and over again. Their failure is the result of "trying hard" to quit - making a decision with their intellect and relying on their willpower to bring it to pass. [9] They are doomed to failure because of what

> **Our trust is so firmly entrenched in our willpower and intellect that whenever we are in need, without thinking we automatically grab those "tools."**

---

[9] In The Bondage of the Will, Martin Luther makes the point that our willpower has no authority in the spiritual realm. He says, "That is to say, man should realize that in regard to his money and possessions he has a right to use them, to do or to leave undone, according to his own 'free-will' - though that very 'free-will' is overruled by the free-will of God alone, according to His own pleasure. However, with regard to God and in all that bears on salvation or damnation, he has no 'free-will,' but is a captive, prisoner and bondslave, either to the will of God, or to the will of Satan" (p.107).

Paul says that to try to keep the Law in our own power sets in motion a curse in the spiritual realm, and Jesus is the only one who can end that curse: *For as many as are of the works of the law are under the curse; for it is written, "Cursed is everyone who does not continue in all things which are written in the book of the law, to do them." But that no one is justified by the law in the sight of God is evident, for "The just shall live by faith." Yet the law is not of faith, but "The man who does them shall live by them." Christ has redeemed us from the curse of the law, having become a curse for us (for it is written, "Cursed is everyone who hangs on a tree.)"* (**Galatians 3:10-13**).

we have just seen about God's laws. This misunderstanding is a big problem, and it is rampant in the Church. The Bible makes very powerful statements regarding the illusion of our will. [10] It is a universal flaw in mankind to think we can manage our own life in our own strength. It is so automatic, insidious, and covert that we don't even realize what we are doing. [11]

We may now be tempted to say, "What's the use? If I can't stop the operation of God's laws which are impelling me to do what I don't want to do, I might as well give up." But there is a way to obey the Lord. We just need to understand the provision that Jesus has made for us and make use of it. Let me give another example.

Another huge truck is speeding down the highway. A traffic jam lies ahead, and the truck driver needs to stop the truck quickly. Does he open the door and drag his foot on the pavement to stop the truck? Of course not. He doesn't have within himself the power to stop the truck. What he does do is to <u>decide</u> to press the brake pedal, and then to <u>act</u> by actually pressing it. This activates a powerful brake system, which has been provided for just such a purpose, and the truck comes to a stop. The driver didn't stop the truck by his own power, but he did need to do the following:

1. <u>Recognize</u> the problem.
2. <u>Believe</u> in the brake system.
3. <u>Decide</u> to activate the system.
4. <u>Act</u> by physically pushing the brake pedal.

---

[10] Romans 7:7-25 makes an especially potent and clear statement regarding the futility of trying to use your willpower to keep the law.

[11] There is a popular teaching that God strengthens our will so that we can obey Him ("The Purpose Driven Life" by Rick Warren, page 180). There is no scriptural basis for this, and this view tends to set us into striving. The Lord wants us to be like Him, not to act like Him.

That was his job as the driver. If he didn't act, there would be a mess. In this same way, in spiritual matters, we have to:

1.<u>Recognize</u> the problem.

2. <u>Believe</u> in the powerful provision Jesus has given us to stop the operation of God's laws against us.

3.Use our willpower to <u>decide</u> to activate the provision.

4.<u>Act</u> by praying.

As you can see, our willpower does have a part to play in our being set free, but it is not the force or power that brings it about. I will elaborate on this process of being set free in the next few chapters.

## God's Laws Bring "Good" or "Bad"

God has provided a system that has sufficient power to stop the operation of God's laws that are bringing destruction, frustration, and failure into our life. However, before we can activate it, we first need to understand more about how God's laws cause us to do the things that we hate.

When God created the spiritual realm, there were two possible ways for a person to exist. If we align our lives with what brings good things (we "obey the Law"), we receive good consequences (blessings). When Adam and Eve walked in the Garden of Eden in obedience to God, life was good.

On the other hand, if we align our lives with what brings bad things (we "disobey the Law"), we experience bad consequences (curses). When Adam and Eve disobeyed God and ate of the tree of the knowledge of good and evil, bad things resulted.

Blessings always flow when we are aligned with His laws. All of us are reaping blessings in certain areas of our life. For example, my son was having financial problems shortly after he graduated from college. He had recently made a decision to follow Jesus, and I spoke to him about tithing. He said, "Dad, how can I give ten percent off the top of my paycheck? I can't pay my bills as it is." But he believed what the Bible said and began to tithe. Immediately, and to my son's astonishment, his financial problems ended. He has continued to tithe, and the Lord has continued to bless his finances. A word of caution is in order. Having money is not always good, and not having money is not always bad. This will become clearer as you read more chapters.

We don't want the blessings to stop. We want more of them. As we align ourselves with the way the spiritual realm is constructed for blessings, we receive blessings. Therefore it is important for us to know how the spiritual realm works for blessing so that we can receive more good.

On the other hand, we also need to understand how the spiritual realm works against us when we sin, so that we can stop the bad things from continuing to happen in our lives.

When we sin, we set in motion God's laws against us. We will surely reap what we sow. We don't sow corn and reap cotton. We don't sow sin and reap blessings. We sow sin and reap bad consequences.

There are, of course, many ways that we can sin, and they all have consequences. [12]

The most destructive consequences are the sinful behaviors that we don't want to do. We are impelled to do them by the operation of God's law, and as a result, our willpower is completely unable to free us

---

[12] **Galatians 5:19-21** gives a partial list of possible sins: *adultery, fornication, uncleanness, licentiousness, idolatry, sorcery, hatred, contentions, jealousies, outbursts of wrath, selfish ambitions, dissentions, heresies, envy, murders, drunkenness, revelries, and the like.*

  **1 Corinthians 6:9-10** lists more sins: *Neither . . . homosexuals, nor sodomites, nor thieves, nor covetous . . . nor extortioners will inherit the kingdom of God.*

  My purpose is not to try to give an exhaustive list of sins, but to give common examples.

from this bondage. [13] Paul reveals the answer to our bondage to these consequences when he writes:

> *O wretched man that I am! Who will deliver me from this body of death? I thank God – through Jesus Christ our Lord!* (Romans 7:24-25).

## The System That Has Enough Power

For us to have victory over the destruction, frustration, pain, and failure in our life, God had to provide a system that had sufficient power. In fact, for us to be set free requires a miracle! [14]

Jesus was sent by the Father to provide a way out for us. He came to take away our sins. His blood is the only cure for sin, and sin is what is causing our problem. When we pray, as we repent, [15] forgive, and are forgiven, Jesus pays off our debt and takes it upon Himself. The negative consequences resulting from the sin will continue into eternity, but Jesus will take over bearing the weight of that, and we are set free. For us, in

---

[13] In fact, trying to stop the operation of God's laws in our life with our own willpower is not just foolish and ineffective, it is sin. "And since all pursuit, even the perverted sort, is, in intention, pursuit of life, this means seeking life where it is not – in the created world. For to deny God as Creator is to turn away from Him to the creation . . . Hence, the ultimate sin reveals itself to be the false assumption of receiving life not as the gift of the Creator but procuring it by one's own power, of living from one's self rather than from God" (Bultmann, Theology of the New Testament, Part II, p. 232)..

[14] Then the question is, how do we become like Jesus? The answer is, it takes a *miracle*. "It means that free, ethical obedience can have its origin only in miracle, quite in keeping with the view that from the fetters of flesh and sin man must be freed to obedience by the deed of God" (Bultmann, Theology of the New Testament, Part II, p.337). We need a legal transaction to take place in the spiritual realm if we are to be like Jesus. So being saved into God's kingdom and being changed into His image are miracles. They are both things that no man can accomplish through his or her own strength and ability.

[15] To repent means, in part, "implying pious sorrow for unbelief and sin and a turning from them unto God and the gospel of Christ . . . Jesus draws a picture of the true penitent person. Such is assured of the forgiveness of the Father" (Zodhiates, The Complete Wordstudy Dictionary, New Testament, p.969).

regard to this particular sin, it is as though we had never committed it. The bad behavior going on in our life as a consequence of our sin ceases to happen.

## The "Blood" And The "Cross"

I will often refer to Jesus' "blood" and His "cross." Some writers admonish us to "take it to the cross," or to "apply the blood." References to "blood" and "cross", either in combination or separately, are short-hand ways of referring to the <u>whole provision</u> that God made for us, through the sacrifice of Jesus, to forgive us our sins and cleanse us from unrighteousness (1 John 1:9). This is activating our sanctification. The provision is God's way of setting us free from our own sin and its consequences which resulted from our following in the footsteps of Adam and Eve.

Even though Jesus paid the penalty for our sin when He died on the cross 2000 years ago, we need to do something to bring the benefits of that provision into our lives. [16] He has offered to pay our debt for us, but we need to accept it in a specific circumstance. We need to apply this provision purposefully to a particular sin for it to have an effect. Only when we take specific action (we pray to repent and are forgiven), do we benefit from the provision He has already made for

> **Since the thing causing our ongoing problem is sin, there is only one cure, and that is the blood and the cross of Jesus.**

forgiveness of our sins. In my previous example, the truck driver had to press the brake pedal to engage the powerful brake system built into the truck. I will write more about how to pray in the next few chapters.

---

[16]    Please note that when I sin, this does not mean I am then going to hell. If that were the case, heaven would be empty, as we all sin and fall short of the glory of God (Romans 3:23). Our sin does have negative consequences, but we will still go to heaven (1 Corinthians 3:15).

Suppose some generous person placed $1,000 in my checking account. When I write a check, I benefit from the money. As long as I don't know about the money being there, or as long as I don't <u>believe</u> it is there, or as long as I don't <u>decide</u> to make a withdrawal and <u>act</u> by writing a check on that account, this money is of no benefit to me. It could remain unused in my account until the day I die. So it is with the gift God gave us in the sacrifice of Jesus. We need to know that the provision is there. We also need to know how to apply it to our real life struggles, and we need to act.

## There Are <u>Two</u> Ways To Stop Bad Behavior

When we recognize undesirable behavior, we have probably thought there was only one way of stopping it. But it should now be clear that there are <u>two</u> ways, because there are <u>two</u> possible sources of the bad behavior, the <u>psychological</u> realm and the <u>spiritual</u> realm. To stop the undesirable behavior we need to use the "tool" that is effectual in that particular realm.

If we have "tried" to change our behavior by using our willpower (psychological realm), but the bad behavior (bad fruit) has continued, we have simply been using the wrong "tool." Since our willpower was ineffective, we now know we are dealing with a spiritual problem and we need to use the appropriate tool - the blood of Jesus. In the past we may have thought the only option available was our willpower.

Our willpower is not trash, nor is it useless. It has a job to do, but its' area of authority is in the psychological realm, not the spiritual realm. Both a watchmaker's screwdriver and a sledgehammer have a purpose. One would not be very successful in splitting wood with a watchmaker's screwdriver, nor be very successful in repairing a watch with a sledgehammer. We need to use the right tool for the job at hand.

See the following page for an illustration of the two alternatives you have at your disposal to stop undesirable behavior.

# Two Alternatives
# For Changing Bad Behavior

Recognize undesirable behavior

Consider two possible sources:

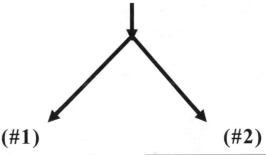

(#1)                                (#2)

| **Psychological Realm** | **Spiritual Realm** |
| --- | --- |
| Habit/impulse | Sin (bad root) |
| ↓ | ↓ |
| Undesirable behavior | Undesirable behavior (bad fruit) |
| ↓ | ↓ |
| Decide to do better | Decide to do better |
| ↓ | ↓ |
| Willpower | Blood of Jesus (become like Him) |

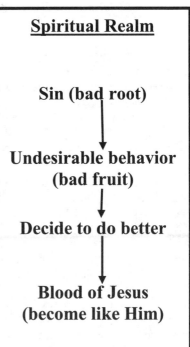

Undesirable behaviors that have their source in the spiritual realm are rigid, compelling, and powerful; and they resist our efforts to overcome them. We are stuck, are at their mercy, and feel defeated. [17] These behaviors that are destructive (what I will call bad behavior, or bad fruit) can either be acts that hurt others, or they can be codependent behaviors that hurt us. See examples of these behaviors in the following footnote.[18]

## "Bad Roots" and "Bad Fruit"

When we sin and plant an area of wounding in our heart, the sin dwelling in that area can be called a "bad root." By their very nature, bad roots produce "bad fruit," whereas "good roots" produce "good fruit."

> *"Even so, every good tree bears good fruit, but a bad tree bears bad fruit. A good tree cannot bear bad fruit, nor can a bad tree bear good fruit. A good tree cannot bear bad fruit, nor can a bad tree bear good fruit. . . Therefore by their fruits you will know them."* (Matthew 7:17-18, 20).

---

[17] **John 8:34-36,** *Most assuredly, I am saying to you, Everyone who habitually commits sin is a slave of sin. But the slave does not abide in the house forever. The Son abides forever. If therefore the Son make you free, you shall be free individuals in reality.* (Wuest). The verb "commit" is the Greek present participle form, which expresses continuous or repeated action. So when we are reaping from a bad root over and over, we are a slave to it - a slave has no choice but to obey his master. But Jesus can set us free from this bondage.

[18] These rigid behaviors come in many forms, and I will list some to illustrate. Perhaps as you scan this list, you will find at least one that applies to you. Addictions are common examples of bad fruit, such as workaholism, gambling, television, computer games, overeating, alcohol, drugs, pornography, promiscuity, adultery. Some bad fruit is relational, such as compulsion to control or manipulate, verbal abuse, blaming others, always being the one that is at fault, lack of intimacy, romance problems, sexual problems, not being thoughtful, not spending time with loved ones, lack of empathy, lack of emotion, hard heartedness, people pleasing, being compelled to be "nice," anger or being passive, being obsessed with one's appearance or what other people will think, fear of meeting new people, lying. Other examples are compulsive behaviors, being greedy or miserly, financial problems or being overly thrifty, being driven by anxiety or fear, occult involvement. Bad fruit is compulsive, rigid, extreme, and beyond our conscious control.

The bad things happening in our lives, including bad behavior, are "bad fruit" from a "bad root." There is no bad fruit without a bad root being present. A bad root <u>always</u> produces bad fruit, and a good root <u>always</u> produces good fruit. The root produces fruit after its own kind. There are no exceptions. Bad behavior <u>never</u> comes from a good root, and good behavior <u>never</u> springs from a bad root.

Bad fruit is compulsive, rigid, extreme, and beyond our conscious control.

## Track Backward From-"Fruit"-To-"Root"

Once you realize that your willpower is impotent to stop the bad behavior, you can recognize that you are dealing with a spiritual problem in your life (bad fruit). Then you must find the source (the bad root). <u>You must track backward from the bad fruit to the bad root</u> (from the behavior to the cause).

The following story illustrates how a person's bad behavior is connected to sin. Mike had an angry father. When Mike was a little boy, his father

> **Bad fruit <u>always</u> comes from a bad root.**

sinned against Mike by abusing him verbally and physically. Mike hated the abuse and judged his father for it. Mike's father used to lose his temper and beat Mike, and much to his dismay, as an adult he found himself losing his temper and beating his own son, just like his father did to him. Mike hates the sinful behavior he is absolutely impelled to do, but he can't stop it, no matter how hard he tries. In truth, he is being impelled to do these sinful things by the operation of God's law. He has a bad root (the Bitter Root Judgment he made as a little boy) that is producing the bad fruit [19] (the present sinful behavior that he hates).

## Once You Identify The "Bad Root," Then Pray

Once you identify the bad root, you need to pray about it. There is no other cure. Without prayer, (repenting and being forgiven) there is no forgiveness of sin. I will talk more about how to appropriate

| Steps for applying Jesus' provision |
| --- |
| 1. **Find the root** |
| 2. **Pray** |

Jesus' provision in **Chapter 6** ("Forgiving Ends These Problems").

When the bad root is gone, a bad tree no longer is present to produce the bad fruit. An apple tree can illustrate this principle. An apple tree bears apples. If we pick the fruit off an apple tree, apples will grow back. The tree will not replace the apples we picked with peaches, but with more apples. When we see an apple, we know that it came from an apple tree, not a peach tree. When the apple tree is removed, there are no more apples produced.

When the bad root is gone, a bad tree no longer exists to produce the bad fruit.

## Isn't "Bad Fruit" Sin?

I have been emphasizing healing bad roots (which are sin), but bad fruit is also sin. Mike's bad root (judging his father) was sin. In addition, his bad fruit (abusing his own son) was also sin, and it needed to be forgiven by Jesus. We need to hate our bad fruit and want it to change. But it is important to understand the difference between the fruit and the root so that the bad behavior stops recurring. In my example, Mike does need

---

[19] In **Hebrews 12:15** the Bible uses the term 'the root of bitterness' for something that can spring up and cause problems and affect many: *looking diligently lest anyone fall short of the grace of God; lest any root of bitterness springing up cause trouble, and by this many become defiled;*

to repent of his current abusive behavior (pick off the fruit); but if he stops there, it will simply happen again (grow back). The only way to stop this cycle he hates is to deal with his childhood judgment against his father (dig up the bad root). I will address this whole process in more detail in Chapters 5, "Judging Causes Problems," and Chapter 6, "Forgiving Ends These Problems."

Since bad fruit <u>always</u> comes from a bad root, and good fruit <u>always</u> comes from a good root, the only way to stop the tree from bearing bad fruit is to remove the bad root and substitute the "good root" (Jesus).

In the Church we have primarily been fruit inspectors, and we have focused on picking off the bad fruit. This is important, since the bad fruit is sin. But we have failed to understand the necessity of removing the bad root, and so we

> **To stop the bad cycle, the blood of Jesus needs to be applied, but to the <u>root</u> rather than just to the fruit.**

have failed in our Christian walk, over and over again: *what I hate, that I do* (Romans 7:15). The provision that Jesus made for removing our sin must be applied to the <u>root</u> and not just to the fruit to be effectual in setting us free.

Please be aware that once our heart has been cleansed by Jesus, and the reaping in the spiritual realm has been stopped, there may still be some residual consequences in the world around us from our previous sins. For instance, Mike's own children will likely still be angry with him and will have judged him for his past abusive behavior towards them. They are therefore wounded and will need to be healed by Jesus. In addition, his past abusive behavior may have led his wife to divorce him. Then, even though he has been healed, his family may remain broken.

# Chapter 4

## Remove All The Bad Roots
### *It Is Possible*

A subtle but profound misunderstanding of what we are like inside has made it difficult for many Christians to see how there can be sin inside themselves. There is a prevalent view that implies that inside we are like a jar, a container with a single compartment. Therefore, when we give our life to Jesus, He forgives our sins and the jar is now clean. Now that we are pure on the inside, we should be able to act pure on the outside.

The reason this view is erroneous is that, unfortunately, this is never the way it works. I know of no one, including myself, for whom life has been this way. And it was not that way for Paul when he wrote the book of Romans (specifically Chapter 7) for us. [20]

The truth is that inside we are more like a honeycomb than a honey jar. We have many compartments inside, not just one. Some of the compartments contain Jesus, and those are like the "good roots" referred to in Scripture, and which I referred to in the prior chapter. These good roots produce good fruit.

> *But the fruit of the Spirit is love, joy, peace, longsuffering, kindness, goodness, faithfulness, gentleness, self-control. . .* (Galatians 5:22-23).

And this good fruit is always produced by good roots.

---

[20] **Romans 7:15-17,** *For what I am doing, I do not understand. For what I will to do, that I do not practice; but what I hate, that I do. If, then, I do what I will not to do, I agree with the law that it is good. But now, it is no longer I who do it, but sin that dwells in me.*

*"Even so, every good tree bears good fruit, but a bad tree bears bad fruit. A good tree cannot bear bad fruit, nor can a bad tree bear good fruit. . . Therefore by their fruits you will know them."* (Matthew 7:17-18, 20).

However, some of the compartments still contain bad roots. These bad roots produce bad fruit, as I have previously mentioned, and they are still present and continue to produce bad fruit even after we become a Christian. These bad roots are shown as dark spots in the following honeycomb diagram.

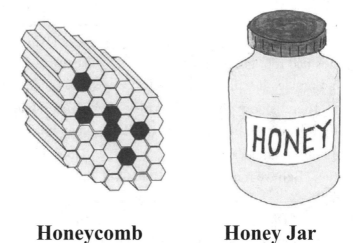

**Honeycomb**          **Honey Jar**

We need to allow Jesus into <u>each</u> compartment of the "Honeycomb" that has darkness in it. This transformation is a process, not a one-time event.

This is the sanctification process which is addressed in so many places in the Bible. Bringing Jesus into each compartment is the process of being changed into His image.

**This transformation is a process, and not a one-time event.**

Once Jesus has taken up residence in that particular place in our "Honeycomb," He produces the good fruit automatically, because Jesus can do nothing but produce good fruit. It is His nature. As He takes over that part of our heart, <u>His nature actually becomes ours</u> in that area, not just positionally (by virtue of our rebirth), but as actual fact. This good root, that now resides in that part of our "Honeycomb", then produces good fruit.

For instance, if we have struggled with lying, we have found that trying hard not to lie hasn't worked (trying implies use of our willpower). We find ourselves still lying. We need to find the bad root. Perhaps we realize that our

> **Jesus' nature actually becomes ours in that particular area in us.**

father lied to us, and we judged him for it (we sinned by judging him). This bad root is causing our bad fruit. When we deal with the bad root and replace it with the life of Jesus, we find we just don't lie anymore. [21] There is now good fruit, which is evidence of Jesus in that place in us. It is now so natural not to lie that we may not even be aware that we are different, because it is a new "us." [22] Does this sound too good to be true? Believe me, it <u>is</u> true. Better yet, believe Jesus when He said,

> *"Therefore you shall **be** perfect, just as your Father in heaven is perfect"* (Matthew 5:48, I added the bold).

---

[21] In the next few chapters I will explain <u>how</u> to take out the bad root and replace it with a good one. Here I am simply showing the <u>necessity</u> for this change to happen.

[22] God will change you inside, and thus cause you do what He does. **Ezekiel 36:27**: *I will put My Spirit within you and cause you to walk in My statutes, and you will keep my judgments and do them.* God will not coerce, compel, or require you to do it, because you can't. He knows He must do it in you. It is not a question of "if" He will do it. It is a question of **"how"** this can become reality in you.

When Jesus cleanses one compartment of the Honeycomb, it does not mean that all the compartments are clean. Other bad roots will undoubtedly remain, and they will be causing other bad fruit. We need to continue being transformed as God shows us areas in our heart that need healing. This is what Paul meant when he said,

> **We need to keep on being transformed as God shows us areas in our heart that need healing.**

> *work out your own salvation with fear and trembling; for it is God who works in you both to will and to do for His good pleasure* (Philippians 2:12-13).

## Ripeness

All of us want to be <u>completely</u> healed and set free <u>right now</u>. Once you discover that healing and relief from your pain and bad fruit is possible, you don't want to wait. You may wonder why this process has to take the rest of your life. Doesn't God want you healed?

You need to be patient. Jesus is directing your sanctification process, and He is proceeding as fast as possible. You are not behind schedule. We may want Him to go faster; but if He is going slowly, you can be assured He is acting slowly for a good reason. For instance, if the bad root relates to a very traumatic event, the memory of the event may be deeply buried. Your defenses buried it specifically so you

> **Jesus is directing your sanctification process.**
>
> **If He is going slowly, it is because that is what is best for you.**

wouldn't have to re-live it. To see it again before you are prepared might cause you to be re-traumatized. Because God loves you, He wants you healed, not wounded further. Before revealing such a root to you, He spends time preparing you. He will not let you see it until you will be able to see it without again being wounded. God's process will have made you ripe to deal with this root.

"Ripeness" is like picking apples. If you try to pick an apple before it is ripe, it is difficult to pull off the tree, and you are likely to damage the branch. However, ripe apples fall off easily in your hand. So the Lord ripens you so that when you pray (when you apply the blood of Jesus), it is easy. Then the process brings healing. But you can't rush your healing any more than you can speed the ripening of the apples on a tree.

## Inside-Out!

*"If you love Me, keep My commandments"* (John 14:15).

When we read a scripture like this, <u>we tend to strive</u> to keep His commandments, because we want to please God. We want Him to know that we love Him, and it seems as though this scripture is telling us that the way we can prove our love for him is to keep His commandments. How can one reconcile this with what we have been discovering about our inability to keep His commandments in our own strength (that is, with our willpower)?

Fortunately, Jesus clearly explains what He meant in the context surrounding the above scripture. The explanation is in John 15:5, which is sandwiched between two scriptures that talk about keeping His commandments.

*"He who has My commandments and keeps them, it is he who loves Me. And he who loves Me will be loved by My Father, and I will love him and manifest Myself to him"* ( John 14:21).

*" I am the vine, you are the branches. He who abides in Me, and I in him, bears much fruit; for **without Me you can do nothing"** (**John 15:5**, I added the bold). .* [23]

*"If you keep My commandments, you will abide in My love, just as I have kept My Father's commandments and abide in His love"* (John 15:10).

What could be clearer than *"without Me you can do nothing?"* Keeping this in mind, then John 15:10 is saying something like, "If you keep My commandments this is <u>evidence</u> that you have been changed into My image, because

> **Our Christian life is meant to be lived from the inside-out, not from the outside-in.**

on your own you could not do it. When you have My nature, you love the Father in exactly the same way that I do." Jesus loves the Father because that is His nature. The reason that we can be thrown into striving to keep God's commandments is that we are confused about how we go

---

[23] **John 15:1-10,** *"I am the true vine, and My Father is the vinedresser. Every branch in Me that does not bear fruit He takes away; and every branch that bears fruit He prunes, that it may bear more fruit. You are already clean because of the word which I have spoken to you. Abide in Me, and I in you. As the branch cannot bear fruit of itself, unless it abides in the vine, neither can you, unless you abide in Me. I am the vine, you are the branches. He who abides in Me, and I in him, bears much fruit; for without Me you can do nothing. If anyone does not abide in Me, he is cast out as a branch and is withered; and they gather them and throw them into the fire, and they are burned. If you abide in Me, and My words abide in you, you will ask what you desire, and it shall be done for you. By this My Father is glorified, that you bear much fruit; so you will be My disciples. As the Father loved Me, I also have loved you; abide in My love. If you keep My commandments, you will abide in My love, just as I have kept My Father's commandments and abide in His love."*

about pleasing God. We focus on our <u>behavior</u> (keeping the commandments) rather than the <u>cause</u> of the behavior (our heart condition). We try to keep the commandments in order to prove that we love God. That is <u>backwards</u>.

We can only please God by first being changed into the image of Jesus in our "Honeycomb," and then we will keep the commandments because that is now our new nature. [24] The heart has to change first, and then the behavior will change. Changing our behavior does not change our heart. [25] 1 John 4:19 says,

*We love him because He first loved us.*

This is the direction of the flow, from God to us, not the other way around. If you are not clear on this, you can misread many scriptures. I

---

[24] **John 15:10,** "*If you keep My commandments, you will abide in My love, just as I have kept My Father's commandments and abide in His love.*" We will do it <u>just like He did</u>. Was the Father's love of Jesus conditioned on His behavior? No, it is clear that Jesus was filled with the Holy Spirit, and what He did was the <u>result</u> of the presence of God in Him. "*Most assuredly, I say to you, the Son can do nothing of Himself, but what He sees the Father do; for whatever He does, the Son also does in like manner*" (John 5:19).

In these scriptures in John in which God's love <u>seems</u> to be conditional, Jesus is actually saying that we will be keeping His commandments <u>as a result</u> of His presence (His love) abiding in us, because it will be an overflow of a heart that has been changed. Then John 15:10 would be saying something like, "He who keeps My commandments (the symptom or good fruit) must have My love abiding in him (the cause or the root), or he couldn't do it."

When Jesus says we should keep His commandments He is simply saying that is how we can tell whether there is a good or a bad root inside.

[25] Our behavior is the <u>evidence</u> of our heart condition, and it actually expresses what is in our heart. But it is not the <u>basis</u>, of our heart condition. (Hulbert, Lesson 68).

would suggest that you read John 14:15 through 15:17 in your Bible to get the full flow of what Jesus is saying. [26]

Let me illustrate this with a parallel. Imagine that I break my leg. It hurts, so I take a painkiller, and it hurts less (I manipulate the symptom). But the leg is still broken (the cause).

> **God's commandments are a way of measuring whether we have a bad root inside.**

If I neglect the painkiller, it hurts a lot. If the doctor said that a healthy leg shouldn't hurt, I would agree. If mine weren't broken, it wouldn't hurt. But saying my broken leg shouldn't hurt doesn't keep it from hurting. The only way for my leg pain to go away (the symptom, or bad fruit) is for my broken leg (the cause, or bad root) to heal (be changed to a good root).

Similarly, when I commit a sin that plants a bitter root, there is a wound in my heart. The bitter root causes emotional pain and I have bad fruit, so I try to act differently (I manipulate the symptom). But it doesn't work very well, because there is a wound, a bad root, inside me (the cause). When Jesus says that I should keep His commandments, I would agree. It is like the doctor saying a healed leg shouldn't hurt. If I didn't have the bad root in my heart, the bad behavior wouldn't happen. But saying I should keep His commandments does not make it possible as long as Jesus isn't abiding in that particular area of my heart (my heart is wounded). The only way I can keep the commandments (the symptom) is for my wounded heart (the cause, or bad root) to be healed and for Jesus to take up residence there (the bad root to be changed to a good root).

-----

[26] Trying hard to obey God in our own strength is sin because we are under the illusion that we can do God's job. We are subtly taking God's place. Hopefully you can now see that when we are reaping bad things in our life it is the consequence of sin. Jesus is the only One who can stop this. This tendency for us to try to keep the Law in our own strength is a subtle and deadly trap. For a more detailed discussion of why trying hard to keep the Law is sin, see "The Primal Sin" on page 96.

The symptom is not the cause. We have had it backwards, and have focused on the symptom (the fruit outside) and not the cause (the root inside).

## Keeping God's Commandments

When Jesus says that we should keep His commandments He is simply saying that is how we can tell whether there is a bad root inside us. Be careful not to be confused about this. The emphasis is <u>never</u> on the fruit, but is always upon the root. Focusing on the bad fruit can set us to striving to keep the commandments with our willpower - and thus doom us to failure. It is a subtle but deadly trap, and we so easily stumble on this stumbling stone. [27]

There are many scriptures that can be misunderstood if we confuse the fruit with the root. The book of James has some significant examples of these kinds of scriptures, such as:

- *Thus also faith by itself, if it does not have works, is dead* (James 2:17).
- *You see then that a man is justified by works, and not by faith only* (James 2:24).

These scriptures are simply saying that if there are no "works" (no good fruit) this is evidence that there is no "faith" (no good root). They are not mandating "trying" with our willpower. Good fruit is all about outward evidence (our behavior), whereas good roots are all about the cause (condition of our heart).

So when we find it difficult to obey a commandment of the Lord, we are stuck in producing "bad fruit." The Apostle Paul describes our

---

[27] *But Israel, pursuing the law of righteousness, has not attained to the law of righteousness. Why? Because they did not seek it by faith, but as it were, by the works of the law. For they stumbled at that stumbling stone* (Romans 9:31-32).

situation: *For what I will to do, that I do not practice; but what I hate, that I do* (Romans 7:15).

## We then have three choices:

1. We can <u>ignore</u> the command.
2. We can <u>try to obey</u> the command in our own strength (our willpower) - - - The Destructive Path shown below.
3. We can have the Lord deal with the bad root through <u>forgiving and being forgiven (apply the blood of Jesus)</u> - - - The Healing Path shown below.

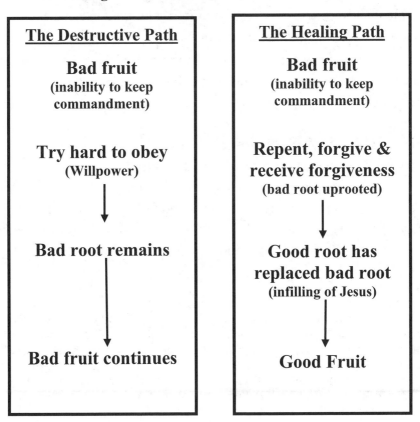

### The Destructive Path

**Bad fruit**
(inability to keep commandment)

**Try hard to obey**
(Willpower)

↓

**Bad root remains**

↓

**Bad fruit continues**

### The Healing Path

**Bad fruit**
(inability to keep commandment)

**Repent, forgive & receive forgiveness**
(bad root uprooted)

↓

**Good root has replaced bad root**
(infilling of Jesus)

↓

**Good Fruit**

## We Plant New Bad Roots

The healing path is to bring Jesus into each bad root in our "Honeycomb." Unfortunately we also frequently plant new bad roots inside.

There are many ways that we all sin and thus plant more bad roots in our "Honeycomb." However, the sin that produces most of the damage and destruction in our lives is the sin of judging. [28] Jesus singled out this sin when He said,

> *"Judge not, that you be not judged. For with what judgment you judge, you will be judged; and with the same measure you use, it will be measured back to you"* (Matthew 7:1-2).

When we judge another, we will surely reap bad consequences. [29] When we plant a bad root in our "Honeycomb" by judging, we can call the bad root a "bitter root" and the action of judging a "Bitter Root Judgment." [30] I will frequently use these terms in the rest of the book. In the next chapter it will become more clear why this particular sin of judging is so serious and so destructive.

## Not Just For A Sick Few

Now that you understand the truth about bad fruit and bad roots, it should be clear that this process is not something for only a few Christians who are really sick emotionally. We all sin and fall short of the glory of God (Romans 3:23), and Jesus died to set all of us free from this bondage. This process of being changed into the image of Jesus, is the normal walk for all Christians.

---

[28] There are many ways that we sin, but the sin that is usually behind all the other sins is the sin of judging. The sin of judging plants the "bitter roots" that compel "bad fruit" (many kinds of sin). This is so because when we judge, we are taking God's place as the judge. Only He gets to do that. We have in us this propensity to want to be like God from the Garden of Eden. See Chapter 8 for more on this propensity. Because it is so central, Rudolf Bultmann calls it the "primal sin." For more on why judging is so central, see page 96.

[29] **Galatians 6:7,** *Do not be deceived, God is not mocked; for whatever a man sows, that he will also reap.*

**Luke 6:37,** *"Judge not, and you shall not be judged. Condemn not, and you shall not be condemned. Forgive, and you will be forgiven."*

Read **Chapter 5**, "Judging Causes Problems," for more on this.

[30] **Hebrews 12:15:** *Lest any root of bitterness springing up cause trouble, and by this many become defiled.*

# Chapter 5

## Judging Causes Problems

### *We All Sin Frequently By Judging*

If I were to comment that my neighbor never mows his lawn and that his yard is always a mess, somebody may say to me, "Don't be so judgmental." Am I judging? Am I sinning? It is certainly important for us to know the answer to these questions so that we can avoid sinning, and thus creating problems for ourselves as a result. Of course there are other sins besides "judging," but this particular sin causes the most problems in our lives.

## There Exists Both "Good" And "Bad" Judging

"Judging" is not always sin. The Bible talks about **four** types of judging. **Three** types are **"good"** judging, and thus are not sin. **One** type is **"bad"** judging, which is sin.

What is confusing is that the Bible uses the same Greek word to refer to all four types, and so one must rely on the <u>context</u> to discern which type is being referred to in a given passage.

**"Good" judging:**

1. **The judging that <u>Jesus does</u>.** Since He is the just and righteous Judge Who has been appointed to this position, He has a right to do this.

2. **The <u>judicial authority</u>** [31] that is to be exercised corporately by the Church in regard to members of the Church. Judging in this context is appropriate and ordained by God.

3. An activity that we **are supposed to** engage in as individual Christians. An English word that would perhaps be more appropriate for this function would be "discernment." We are to <u>use wisdom</u> and to <u>exercise discernment</u>. It is not only permissible to see the negative in a situation or a person, we are encouraged to do so.

4. **"Bad" (sinful) judging**

   The fourth type of judging is the type of judging that we are <u>not</u> supposed to do as individual Christians. This type of judging by us is sin. When we do this type of judging, we are seeing the negative in a situation or a person, but <u>we are also setting ourselves up as the judge, jury, and hangman</u>. [32]

---

[31] **1 Corinthians 5:12-13,** *For what have I to do with judging those also who are outside? Do you not judge those who are inside? But those who are outside God judges. Therefore "put away from yourselves that wicked person."* The whole section, 1 Corinthians 5:1-6:9, concerns this issue.

[32] **Matthew 7:1-2,** *Judge not, that you be not judged. For with what judgment you judge, you will be judged; and with the same measure you use, it will be measured back to you.*

    **Luke 6:37,** *Judge not, and you shall not be judged. Condemn not, and you shall not be condemned. Forgive, and you will be forgiven.*

    **Romans 14:4,** *Who are you to judge another's servant? To his own master he stands or falls. Indeed, he will be made to stand, for God is able to make him stand.*

    **James 4:11-12,** *Do not speak evil of one another, brethren. He who speaks evil of a brother and judges his brother, speaks evil of the law and judges the law. But if you judge the law, you are not a doer of the law but a judge. There is one Lawgiver, who is able to save and to destroy. Who are you to judge another?*

## The Sinful Judging Is Destructive

There are, of course, many ways we can sin. However, of all the sins that we commit, this "bad" judging is the sin that causes the most problems in our lives. When we find ourselves doing the things that we hate, the root that is causing this bad fruit is almost always a judgment.

> . . . *lest any root of bitterness springing up cause trouble, and by this many become defiled* (Hebrews 12:15).

Considering the size of the problem this sin causes, surely it must be a very serious issue.

The problem has its source in the Garden of Eden. When the serpent said, *"For God knows that in the day you eat of it your eyes will be opened, and you will be like God, knowing good and evil"* (Genesis 3:5). Adam and Eve took this bait because something inside of them wanted to be like God. Satan knew all about this sin, because this was also his big transgression.

Therefore, when we judge another we are <u>taking the place of Jesus</u>, and of course this is a very serious transgression. Jesus is the only one who has the right to judge. So when we judge, we are usurping God's place. [33] When we do this, we are violating the first Great Commandment: *You shall love the Lord your God with all your heart, with all your soul, and with all your mind* (Matthew 22:37). There is only one God, and it isn't us! We are doing the judging because we do not trust God to take care of us and to hold others accountable when they trespass against us (and therefore wound us). We feel we must take the

---

[33] **James 4:11-12,** *He who speaks evil of a brother and judges his brother, speaks evil of the law and judges the law. But if you judge the law, you are not a doer of the law but a judge. There is one Lawgiver who is able to save and to destroy. Who are you to judge another?*

    **Romans 14:4,** *Who are you to judge another's servant? To his own master he stands or falls.*

law into our own hands; because if we don't do it, we believe that nobody will.

All major problems in our human life have their roots in the Garden of Eden, and in the two great commandments of Jesus. [34] God has truly explained spiritual reality to us in such simple terms!

## Our Weakness

Why do we all judge so quickly? It is a part of our fallen nature ( I discuss this aspect of our nature in Chapter 8, "The Bad Part Of You". When we perceive that we have been wounded, we always automatically react with bitterness, judgment, and blame. For instance, picture yourself in your kitchen cutting up a carrot. The phone rings, and you lose your concentration and cut your finger instead of the carrot. What is your immediate response? Do you blame the carrot? Do you blame the dull knife? Do you blame your spouse for not sharpening the knife? Do you blame the person who called you? Or do you blame yourself, saying something like this, "You dummy. Why weren't you paying more attention to what you were doing?"

---

**Stop for a minute and think about what your response would be.**

---

Blaming myself, which is judging myself, was always my typical response.

---

[34] **Matthew 22:36-40,** "*Teacher, which is the great commandment in the law?*" *Jesus said to him, "You shall love the Lord your God with all your heart, with all your soul, and with all your mind. This is the first and great commandment. And the second is like it: You shall love your neighbor as yourself. On these two commandments hang all the Law and the Prophets."*

Why couldn't the cut finger just be something that happened? Why did somebody or something have to be at fault? The answer is because it is our fallen nature to judge. <u>This is the problem</u>. Daily we plant numerous roots of bitterness. Since life in this fallen world entails lots of wounding, we do a lot of judging. It is automatic, and we have done it before we consciously know it. Because we have planted many roots of bitterness, we are reaping much bad fruit. Tragically, as long as we walk this earth, we will never lose this tendency to automatically react to wounding with bitterness, judgment and blame. This tendency is an integral part of our fallen human nature.

In the church, there have been controversies about this tendency to sin, and what to call it. The term "flesh" is the most common term in the New Testament, but this word can be confusing. The Greek word translated into English as "flesh" is *sarx* (Strong's # 4561). What is confusing is that sometimes *sarx* means something bad, but sometimes it does not. For example, my right thumb is "flesh," but it has no moral significance. In order to avoid this confusion, I am going to coin my own term for when *sarx* is referring to this tendency to judge (take God's place as judge). I will call this tendency our **"God-wannabe."**

## Our "God-Wannabe" Arrives

When Adam and Eve disobeyed God and ate of the tree of the knowledge of good and evil, bad things resulted.

Satan's temptation was:

> *"For God knows that in the day you eat of it your eyes will be opened and <u>you will be like God"</u>* (Genesis 3:5, underlining is mine).

When Adam and Eve ate of the forbidden fruit, there was planted in mankind <u>a tendency to want to take God's place</u>. This impulse is exactly what got Satan kicked out of heaven.

This tendency to want to take God's place and to run our own lives still exists in all of humanity, because we are descendants of Adam and Eve.

We take God's place whenever we judge another.

> *Judge not, and you shall not be judged. Condemn not, and you shall not be condemned. Forgive, and you will be forgiven* (Luke 6:37).

We all judge, and we do it often. If you think you don't do it, there is one sure way to discover the truth. Ask yourself, do you do the things that you hate to do? Is there bad fruit in your life? If there is bad fruit, there are roots of bitterness in you.

Fortunately, you now have a way to clean up the mess. As often as you judge, you can forgive and be forgiven. The bad root can be pulled out as soon as it is planted.

## How Can You Tell The Difference?

How can you tell if the judging you have just done is good or bad? At first glance this may seem terribly confusing. Fortunately, the Lord has provided a very simple way to tell the difference.

Suppose I live in a small town and I am thinking about going into business with a certain man. I check around and find out that this person has a reputation for being dishonest, and so I decide not to go into business with him. I have judged (discerned) as I am supposed to do.

Alternatively, suppose I live in the small town and I am thinking about going into business with a certain man. Without first checking around and discovering his reputation, I go into business with him. After the business starts I discover that he is not honest. By the time I can get myself out of the business deal it has cost me $100,000. I am now in possession of the same information (that he isn't honest) as in the first example, but you can be sure that in this situation I have done the bad type of judging. How can I tell that I have done the bad judging? Every time I think about that "jerk" I feel like strangling him. Every time I think of him I become very angry and upset. He wounded me, and I judged him for it.

On the other hand, in the first example, I am probably not upset with the man, because I didn't judge him wrongly. After all, he didn't wound me. I am at peace.

How can I tell whether I have judged someone in the way that I am not supposed to? I feel it. I can absolutely feel the bitterness of the bitter root that has been planted in my "honeycomb."

When I realize that I have judged him in the way that I am not supposed to, I can forgive him and be forgiven by Jesus (see **Chapter 6** on forgiving). Then I no longer feel like calling him a "jerk."

## A "Splinter"

We can feel the planting of a bitter root, because there is built into us a sensitivity to wounding in our heart. A parallel to this would be when we get a splinter in our finger. There is built into us a sensitivity to physical wounding. When a splinter gets lodged in our finger, we know it is there because we feel it. When we remove the splinter, our body will know that and will tell us by a feeling of relief of the discomfort. Likewise, when we remove the bitter root, our heart will know that and will tell us (if we are listening) by a feeling of peace in place of the bitterness.

## Denial

Most of the time we can tell whether we have judged another person by the feeling. However, there are times when we will not feel bitterness towards the one who wronged us. When a wound we have received is particularly severe, we may have built a defense to protect us from feeling the pain related to it. For instance, a girl may have been abused by her father, and yet have no sense of her rage towards him. The pain she felt at the time was too big to live with, so she cut herself off from the feeling. We call this sort of defense mechanism "denial." She truly does not even know she is angry inside. However, it will still be possible to discover there is a Bitter Root Judgment inside. In this sort of situation, because the wounding was large, there will be "bad fruit" in her life that will indicate the presence of a "bad root;" and so she can track backwards from the "bad fruit" to the "bad root."

## Perceived Wounding

I have made the statement that we always automatically respond to perceived wounding with bitterness, judgment, and blame. It doesn't matter whether the other person actually, factually, wounded us. What counts is that we feel that they did.

For instance, suppose I was abandoned by my parents when I was a small child. This is a real wounding, and has made me sensitive to abandonment. Then as an adult, suppose a friend of mine declines to go to a ballgame with me, telling me he is too tired. I feel abandoned and judge him, because it seems to me he was making an excuse. Later I find out the friend was coming down with the flu, and he really had wanted to go to the game with me.

There was no actual wound inflicted by my friend, but I wrongly perceived there was, so I judged. My prior wounds and judgments make me more sensitive, and they affect how I perceive and react to other peoples' behavior.

As the Lord heals these wounded areas, I will react less often, because I will perceive less wounding less often. However, this change should not be confused with my built in God-wannabe's tendency to react with bitterness, judgment and blame. I don't react less now because that tendency has gone away or is being healed. I react less because I perceive wounding less often. The next time I am actually wounded by someone, I

**It is therefore important to realize that what is going wrong in our life is not because of what others did to us, but it is because of our bitter reaction to what they did.**

will discover that my tendency to judge has not gone away, because I will again find myself judging. The sequence that occurs is as follows: My friend declines my invitation. I perceive that I have been wounded (abandoned). This automatically triggers my judging, which plants a root of bitterness in my heart. I then feel abandoned, making me aware, after the fact, that the root of bitterness has been planted inside.

Unfortunately, the more bad roots we have, the more bad fruit we have. This is why "judging" is so damaging to us. To make matters worse, the longer a bad root grows inside us, the bigger it gets, the more entrenched it is, and the more difficult it is to eradicate. The bigger the root, the more pervasive is the bad fruit.

## It Is God's Mercy That We Feel Emotional Pain!

If we did not feel the emotional pain, we wouldn't know there is something wrong inside, and the sin would remain in us. When we die, we will go to the Great White Throne Judgment, and there all our sins will be placed before us. Scripture doesn't tell us what the negative consequences will be, but there is a strong implication that we would be better off without those sins. <u>Since the sins that have been washed away by Jesus during our lifetime will not be there, we won't have to pay the price for them at the last judgment</u>. Because the Lord takes the long view, including eternity, He wants to have the opportunity to forgive our sins here, in this life, before we face the Last Judgment. Of course, our unforgiven sins will not keep us out of heaven. We will still be saved, but we will suffer loss. [35]

We do not know when our life on earth will end. But as time goes by the end of our life draws nearer. It therefore becomes more and more urgent that we give our sins to Jesus. God therefore increases the pain, and our burdens get harder to carry until we get desperate enough to seek the cause. We need to forgive now so we won't have to pay later.

## God Changes Us Into His Image

I have talked about the place of our willpower, and the fact that in Western culture our willpower has been placed upon the throne of our lives. This view is so subtle, pervasive, and automatic that it can sneak into our thinking undetected. For example, some Bible teachers try to explain that the way to walk out the Christian life is for God to strengthen our will so that we can obey. These teachers believe that our willpower is the tool to bring victory. But what God intends is for us to be changed into His image. It is a miracle. When He removes a bitter root and comes to live in that place in us, obeying Him is automatic and effortless. In fact, it is so effortless that we may not even realize that we are behaving differently. The good root produces good fruit, because it can do nothing else.

---

[35] **1 Corinthians 3:9,13-16,** *For we are God's fellow workers; you are God's field, you are God's building . . . each one's work will become manifest; for the Day will declare it, because it will be revealed by fire; and the fire will test each one's work, of what sort it is. If anyone's work which he has built on it endures, he will receive a reward. If anyone's work is burned, he will suffer loss; <u>but he himself will be saved</u>, yet so as through fire. Do you not know that you are the temple of God and that the Spirit of God dwells in you?* Here "work" does not refer to "effort," but to the product. Your character is the product, the "building" (verse 9) the "temple" (verse 16). Underlining is mine.

# Chapter 6

# Forgiving Ends These Problems

## *Jesus Can Set You Free*

## Forgiveness Is Essential

We have seen that "judging" is what plants the bitter roots in our heart that causes us to have bad fruit in our lives. This is a serious condition, and we need a way to be set free from the influence of these bitter roots. Forgiving and being forgiven by God is the cure. It is the only way that the bitter root is pulled out and replaced by a good root, which is the presence of Jesus in us.

God has told us a great deal about why forgiveness is essential.

1. Forgiveness is important because God said so. Jesus is the only Judge of the universe. When we judge, we attempt to take His place. God is not happy about this.

2. Forgiveness is important for us. When we judge another, we sin and this plants a bitter root in our heart. This bitter root will produce bad fruit. There is only one cure for this, and that is the forgiveness in Jesus. He shed His blood to take away our sins.

> **Forgiveness is the only way we can be changed into the image of Jesus.**

We need His blood to wash away this sin of judging so we don't have to reap the resulting consequences that come about from the operation of God's laws. The only way to accomplish this is to forgive (from our heart) the one who wounded us, and then to be forgiven by Jesus. When He forgives us, He pays the debt we owe in the spiritual realm, and we are set free from the consequences we would otherwise have to pay for our debt. [36] If we don't forgive (from our heart), we won't be forgiven by God (though this sin will not send us to hell). [37] If we are not forgiven by God, we will continue to do the things we hate (we will continue to experience the reaping from the operation of God's laws). There simply is no other way to be set free.

The consequences of sin are so overwhelmingly too large for us to stop that we need something from outside the natural course of this world to set us free: in other words, a miracle. [38] What Jesus does for us when He provides forgiveness of sin is such a miracle. It is a legal transaction that occurs in the spiritual realm, and it washes away the debt we owe and removes the bitter root inside us. Once the bitter root has been removed, and Jesus has moved into that place in our heart, good fruit begins to grow from this new good root. [39]

---

[36] **Galatians 1:3-4,** *Grace to you and peace from God the Father and our Lord Jesus Christ, who gave Himself for our sins, that He might deliver us from this present evil age, according to the will of our God and Father.*

   **Hebrews 9:28,** *so Christ was offered once to bear the sins of many.*

   **1 John 2:2,** *And He Himself is the propitiation for our sins, and not for ours only but also for the whole world.*

[37] **Matthew 18:35,** *"So My heavenly Father also will do to you if each of you, from his heart, does not forgive his brother his trespasses."*

   **Mark 11:25,** *"And whenever you stand praying, if you have anything against anyone, forgive him, that your Father in heaven may also forgive you your trespasses."*

   **Luke 6:37,** *"Judge not, and you shall not be judged. Condemn not, and you shall not be condemned. Forgive, and you will be forgiven."*

   **Ephesians 4:32,** *And be kind to one another, tenderhearted, forgiving one another, just as God in Christ also forgave you.*

[38] The biblical concept of a miracle is that of an event which runs counter to the observed processes of nature (Elwell, <u>Evangelical Dictionary of Theology</u>, p.723).

[39] See Matthew 12:33-35 and Luke 6:43-45.

# What Does It Mean To Forgive?

There are two common obstacles that often make it difficult for us to forgive. The first obstacle is that we misunderstand what God meant by "forgive." "Forgive" is a word that is so common among Christians that we think we know what it means. However, most of us were taught what this word means by the world around us, and so the meaning we have attached to it may not be the same as what God is referring to when He tells us to forgive. Sometimes this misunderstanding gets in the way of our being able to forgive others in the process of our healing.

For instance, many of us have heard something like, "Forgive and forget." We try to do that, and we find we can't forget what the person did to us. Then we think we haven't forgiven. Or perhaps somebody has hurt us, and we may believe that forgiving means we need to again make ourselves vulnerable to that person. Then something inside us resists forgiving, because we are sure the person will wound us again. Then we find it difficult to forgive.

However, God loves you and He will not ask you to do something that is not good for you, or is dangerous or destructive to you. Once you understand what God meant when He told you to forgive, you will find it much easier to forgive from your heart. Your misunderstanding of what it means to forgive may have been keeping you in bondage.

# What Forgiveness Is <u>NOT</u>

Forgiveness is **not** the following:

1. It is not saying the person did not transgress or hurt us, when he or she in fact did.
2. It is not relieving the other person of their responsibility, such as making excuses for their actions. For example, "My parents couldn't help it," or "They did the best they could," or "I'd have done the same thing if I had been in their shoes."

3. It is not forgetting what the other person did. We can't forget, but the hurt can be removed from the memory, and we can be forgiven for our judging.

4. It is not trusting the other person again when he or she is still unsafe – becoming vulnerable to the person again may not be wise.

5. It is not a "feeling." Rather, forgiving is a decision. However, when forgiveness has been accomplished we will feel differently about the other person whenever we think of them.

6. It is not saying or pretending we weren't hurt and/or that we weren't angry; or ignoring the hurt feeling because we aren't supposed to be angry. Rather, we need to process our feelings, not suppress them.

## What Forgivess IS

Forgiveness is deciding not to hold the other person in debt. [40] Unforgiveness says, "You unjustly hurt me, and you owe me a debt. I will make you pay." Forgiveness says, "Even though you hurt me and owe me a debt, I am writing it off. You owe me nothing. It is not my place to make you pay, and I release you to the judgment of Jesus. He is the just Judge, and He will rightly decide the case. If there is any penalty, He will collect it." [41] Forgiveness does not say, "Go get 'em, God. You

---

[40] Grace means: "graciousness (as gratifying) of manner or act (abstract or concrete) literally, figuratively, or spiritually; especially the divine influence upon the heart, and its reflection in the life: including gratitude" (Strong's, p.77). The second meaning of the verb is to forgive! (C. Brown, The New International Dictionary of New Testament Theology, Vol 2, p.122).

It appears that when we forgive, we are connecting with (or acting like, or coming into unity with) God's nature rather than man's nature (the tendency to respond to perceived wounding with bitterness, judgment, and blame).

". . . 'dead through our trespasses, made alive together with Christ, by grace (*chariti*) you have been saved' (2:5); 'by grace . . . through faith . . . the gift of God' in opposition to 'not your own doing . . . not because of works, lest any man should boast' (2.8f)" (C. Brown, Vol 2, p.122, commenting on Ephesians 2:5-2:8ff).

[41] **Romans 12:19,** *Beloved, do not avenge yourselves, but rather give place to wrath; for it is written, "Vengeance is Mine, I will repay" says the Lord. Therefore if your enemy hungers, feed him; if he thirsts, give him a drink; for in so doing you will heap coals of fire on his head.*

make him pay." Such a statement clearly reveals bitterness still lodged in the heart.

## A Second Obstacle To Forgiving

In addition to misunderstanding what forgiveness really is, there may be a second obstacle to forgiving. We may fear that if we give up our resentment we won't be protected. We may believe that a wall of resentment will protect us. This is, of course, a lie. Holding the resentment causes us to suffer. Later in life we will then struggle with trusting God to be our protector. But in reality, He is the only one who can protect us.

## We Are The Ones Who Suffer

If we do not forgive, we are the ones who suffer. God is a just judge, which means that no one ever gets away with anything, ever, anywhere. Not everyone believes this, but it is true. The law of God is inescapable, and whatever we sow, we will surely reap,

> *Do not be deceived, God is not mocked; for whatever a man sows, that he will also reap* (Galatians 6:7). [42]

## Remove Bitter Roots Immediately!

Bitter roots are easier to eradicate if we remove them soon after they are planted. The longer they are allowed to grow, the larger the root system becomes and the more difficult they are to pull out. Gardeners

---

[42] Note that this is not an exception to the fact that God protects us in ways we don't know. We may be protected from reaping from some of our sins while we are here on earth, but all our unrepented sins will be placed before us at the Great White Throne judgment. We will still be saved, though we will suffer loss (1 Corinthians 3:15). Exactly what "loss" means is not explained in the Bible, but God knows. Since He loves us, He wants to protect us from this "loss." That is why He is so diligent in getting us to repent of our sins during our lifetime here on earth. He takes the long, eternal view.

understand this. When a weed first comes up in a garden, it is small and frail. It can be plucked out easily. However, if one neglects the garden for some time, pulling the weeds is a big job. The roots of the weeds have then become large and entrenched, and sometimes a large hole has to be dug in order to remove them. Healing is easier if you remove a bitter root as soon as it is planted.

Another thing happens if we neglect to keep up with our "weeding." If we allow the sins to pile up, eventually they become too obvious to ignore. People who have lived in the country know what a septic tank is. It is a big cement tank buried underground into which the

> **Because forgiving is so important, we need to remove every obstacle that prevents us from accomplishing it, and we need to be diligent in accomplishing it.**

wastewater from a house runs. There the waste goes through a natural process of cleansing, but some types of waste stay in the tank and gradually fill it up. Periodically it needs to be pumped out, or it overflows and makes a smelly mess. Our hearts are a bit like septic tanks. If we don't keep our own pumped out, it eventually fills up with junk, overflows and makes a mess. It is therefore important that we pump ours out every time some waste enters it. In other words, we need to forgive every time we judge so that our own "septic tank" (our heart) stays clean.

## Who Do We Need To Forgive?

There are probably many people we need to forgive. Psychotherapy and Christian counseling have both tended to focus on relationships with our parents and our siblings. Without a doubt these relationships were impactful, and the roots of bitterness resulting from being wounded by them causes major problems for us. But we frequently judge other people, such as the other driver, the rude waitress, etc.

We can also judge inanimate objects. I frequently judge my computer. I need to forgive and be forgiven by the Lord. That may sound stupid, because my computer has no life. But when I judge, the problem is in me, not the computer; and so I can have a bitter root towards my computer.

However, the deepest hurts, the greatest emotional pain, and the most devastating fruit comes from <u>judging God</u> and <u>judging ourselves</u>.

## Elements For Accomplishing Forgiveness

There are certain elements involved in walking through the process of forgiving when we have judged:

1. **Recognition:** First, we need to recognize that we have judged (sinned). Denial and fear can often interfere with our ability to see what we have done.
2. **Confession:** Then we need to confess that we have sinned. Speak to God verbally about this whole process.
3. **Repentance:** This means to turn away from the sin. We need to hate the sin and want to no longer repeat it.
4. **Forgiveness:** We need to make a decision to forgive, and then forgive from our heart.
5. **Accept forgiveness** from God. Sometimes another person needs to verbalize to us that God has forgiven us before we are able to accept this fact.
6. **Ask the Lord to fill** that place in our heart with His presence. We need Him to take up residence in that place that had previously contained bitterness, judgment, and blame.
7. **Ask the Lord to bless** the other person. If we find this difficult to do, then it is likely that forgiveness has not been fully accomplished.
8. **Restitution:** Sometimes we need to do something extra for the other person, to walk an extra mile. Our relationship with the Lord has already been restored through prayer, but in some situations we need

to do something for the other person in order to restore our relationship with them.  This is the purpose of restitution.  It will bless the other person if you feel led to do this.

## How To Pray

Forgiveness must come from the <u>heart</u> to be effectual:

*So My heavenly Father also will do to you if each of you, from his heart, does not forgive his brother his trespasses* (Matthew 18:35).

> **It is always important that we forgive from our heart as the living Lord leads, rather than recite a rote prayer.**

 Jesus always looks on the heart, not the behavior, and we can't fool Him. Therefore it is always important that we pray as we feel led by the living Lord, and <u>NOT</u> simply recite a rote prayer, as though it were a magical formula.

## The Importance Of Words

Please be aware of the important position that words have in our prayers of forgiveness.  For some reason, God set up the universe in such a way that words have power. *Then God said, "Let there be light," and there was light* (Genesis 1:3).  The words that I speak bring my thoughts into reality.  Once they are spoken, it is as though a legal contract has been signed, or a legal event has happened, in the spiritual realm.  The words can be "bad" and bring about difficulty (for example judging), or they can be "good" and bring about life (for example blessing someone). Though the Bible doesn't explain to us why words have power, it does make the fact abundantly clear, that they do have great power.

## Sample Prayer

A prayer regarding your dad might go something like this:

"Father God, I come to You in the blessed name of Jesus.

I realize that I have judged my father, and I have inside me a root
   of bitterness.

I am sorry that I did this, and I don't want that awful thing in me
anymore.

Dad, I forgive you for _____(the offense).

Lord, I ask you to forgive me for judging and thus planting this root
   of bitterness.

Forgive me for taking Your place as the judge.

I ask you to come into that place in me, remove that ugly thing from
      me and wash me clean with your blood.  Cleanse me in
      every place where that bitterness existed.

Lord, I ask you to come into that place and fill all those places
      with Your presence.

Lord, I ask that you would bless my Dad.

Amen.


But please do not simply recite this as a rote prayer.  Just speak what the
Lord gives you to say.

## How Do You Know You Have Forgiven?

The way you can then tell if you have accomplished forgiveness is to
listen inside to how you feel.  If the bitterness is gone, you did it.  If not,
you may have to pray some more.  God is faithful, and will let you know
if you are finished with this issue.  At that point you will feel peace.  Read
Chapter 7 for more on how your emotions can help you.

## Entrusting God With Our Behavior

The truth is that good behavior (fruit) can only come from a good root inside, not from my striving. Unfortunately, it is not easy for us to entrust God with the job of changing our behavior.   Let me explain.

We all have a tendency to distrust whatever we cannot control. Since we cannot control our inner life (that which is below our level of consciousness), we distrust whatever comes up from inside us.   We believe that we need to be the watchman who monitors and controls our behavior.  We also tend to be under the illusion that we can decide what we want to do, and then accomplish it.   In fact, many of us have been misled by the church to believe that any bad behavior is a conscious "choice" we made.

Most of us have tried to live like this, and have discovered major areas of our lives where this has not worked.  Most of us haven't known about another way to live that does work.

I have just been writing about the alternative.   This new way involves recognizing that this persistent bad behavior comes from bad roots (roots of bitterness) in our "Honeycomb," and that good behavior comes from good roots.   It requires recognition that only the blood of Jesus, and not our effort, can change us.   Therefore, the only way to have enduring good behavior is to remove the bad roots by forgiving and being forgiven, and then to invite the Holy Spirit to come into those places (to become a good root inside us).

Unfortunately, you will likely find it to be very uncomfortable to abandon the old philosophy and live life in the new way.  It is foreign to all of us, and requires a lot of trust.  It is important for you to recognize that you will have to wrestle with this difficulty.  We all do.  But be assured that the blood of Jesus works.

# Chapter 7

# Emotions Are Your Guide

## *So You Can Know What Is Happening Inside*

Suppose you are in your car and you are in a hurry. You get stopped at a stoplight (of course, it always happens when you are in a hurry). The light finally changes to "green" and the driver in front of you does not notice it. He just sits there. What would you do? Likely, you would honk your horn. How would you feel? Wouldn't you be a bit upset? When the other car finally gets going, it is too late for you to get through the light. You then have to wait until the light turns green again. Now you are more than a little upset. How long would it take you to calm down? What would you do to calm yourself down?

We all have developed ways of dealing with our negative emotions by trial and error. We try something and it brings a bit of relief, so we add that to our repertoire as a way to deal with such unpleasant moments in the future. Still, for most of us our emotions are a bit mysterious, we don't know what to do with them, and likely we have only been modestly successful in dealing with them.

As a child I learned to avoid my negative emotions if at all possible. This was the message that I got from living in my family, and it was the method of dealing with emotions that I observed in my parents. My experience is not unusual, because our culture (and unfortunately some of the Church) say that our emotions are unreliable. Regardless of how we try to ignore them, they persist. They come and go in a seemingly mysterious way, in a way that we do not find ourselves able to adequately control. Negative emotions are a "problem" we all share.

## What Are Emotions?

Are emotions simply random? Are they unpredictable? Did God make a mistake when He gave them to us? Or were they useful before Adam and Eve sinned but are now corrupted by The Fall? Are some of them "bad?" Is it a sin to feel selfish? Is it a sin to feel jealous? Is it a sin to feel angry?

**Your negative emotions are your friend. They are simply messages from inside warning you that there is a problem.**

I have a burglar alarm in my home. On a couple of occasions I have accidentally set it off, and the sound the loud speaker made was earsplitting. The pain was unbearable. I had to do something right away to escape the pain. So I plugged my ears with my fingers and went to the keypad and entered the code. Then the alarm immediately stopped, so the pain stopped. But what would I do if I didn't know the code? My fingers in my ears were only mildly successful in reducing the pain, so I would have to do something else. I could leave and wait outside until the noise stopped (and the police came). Or I could find the loudspeaker and cover it over with something. That would likely not work any better than covering my ears. Better yet, I could cut the wire to the loud speaker. That would stop the noise.

The purpose of the alarm was to make known an intrusion into my house. If the alarm had been set off by a burglar instead of by me, that would be important information. If a burglar entered and I did not have an alarm, something really bad might happen. The burglar alarm was purposely designed to be impossible to ignore, because it is important that the "intrusion" stop. The neighbors and the police need to be alerted, and the intruder needs to know they have been discovered so they will stop doing their dirty work.

Our negative emotions are like that. Some of our emotions are "earsplittingly" hurtful, because they are giving us very important information that we must not ignore. For instance, when you are in front of a group of people and you tell a joke and nobody laughs, you may feel a strong rush of shame, and your face may turn red. Or suppose a large dog rushes towards you, growling and showing its teeth. You will likely feel a large surge of fear go through you. Fortunately not all our negative emotions are that severe. God designed them to be proportional to the bad news they are giving us.

You also have pleasant emotions which were given to you so that you would be attracted to whatever is making you feel good. What makes you feel good are the things that fulfill the many needs you have, such as the need for love, affirmation, sex, etc.

## "Feelings" and "Emotions"

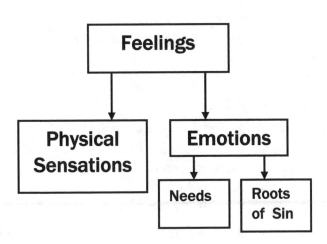

We receive various signals from inside us (see diagram on page 113). Some of these signals relate to the physical status of our body, and some of them relate to our psychological/spiritual status. When I use the term "feelings," I am including both categories. When I use the term "physical sensations" I am referring to the physical signals. And when I use the term "emotions" I am referring to the psychological/spiritual signals.

"Emotions" can be telling us about unmet psychological needs ("I need a hug"), or the presence of a root of sin, usually a Bitter Root Judgment.

"Physical sensations" and "emotions" have a great deal in common, and the purpose of all of our "feelings" is to make us consciously aware of something that is going on below our level of consciousness. Most of us do not have difficulty understanding our "physical sensations" (for instance I am thirsty, or my feet hurt), but our problems tend to arise from misunderstanding our "emotions." Because of the similarities between "physical sensations" and "emotions," I will often use parallels between them to clarify a point I am making about "emotions."

If God had not given your "feelings" to you, you would not have any way of knowing the status of what is going on inside of you. You would not know what your needs are, and so you would have no way of fulfilling them. If you did not feel thirst, you would not drink something, and then you would die.

## Your Treasure Inside

We each have within us a part of us that is made in God's image. It is the "real" us, and he or she is good. That part of us resides below our level of consciousness, so we need a way to hear what that part of us is saying to help us through life. For clarity, I have given that part of us the label "Treasure Inside." See Chapter 9, "The Good Part of You" for a detailed discussion of this aspect of your being. Our emotions are a powerful communication system that our Treasure Inside uses to speak to us.

## Our Attempts At Bringing Peace

As a child I knew what to do when I had a physical need. When I was thirsty, I got a drink. However, I didn't know the "code" to turn off the emotional pain. When strong negative emotions came to me I had to find a way to reduce the pain. It was as if I started out by "plugging my ears" (I tried to ignore the message). Since that was only modestly helpful, I searched for a more effective means. I could not "leave," because the noise was in me. So eventually I "cut the wire" (I made an Inner Vow, a deep spiritual decision, not to hear), and then the pain stopped.

## The Wall

To shut out the pain, I essentially had built a "wall" to block out my emotions. Throughout this book I will be referring to this mechanism as "The Wall," and explaining more about it.

> **When in emotional pain, we build "The Wall" to escape it.**

Unfortunately, then the "intrusion" (the cause of the emotional pain) had not been fixed, and so the "burglar" had not been dealt with. Cutting the wire, or anything else I would do to reduce my sensitivity to my negative emotions, had bad side effects. Not hearing the alarm going off, I would not know when a "burglar" came inside and was doing his destructive work.

When I was a boy I had a friend whose father had experienced a stroke, and he had lost the feeling on one side of his body. One day my friend and his father and I were standing in their basement and we smelled something burning. It was his father's hand! He was leaning against the furnace. Since he could not feel the heat, he did not withdraw his hand, and he was badly burned. The physical pain that I feel when I touch something hot is my friend, because it motivates me to stop the pain. I quickly remove my hand from the hot surface, and thus I limit the damage to my body. Physical pain is my friend.

My emotional pain is just like that. Bad things happen when I can no longer clearly hear my negative emotions, because I have built The Wall inside. [43] Then, when something bad happens inside, I will not know about it. Using my metaphor, because I do not know the "burglar" is there, he is free to do his damaging work inside. I will not know about his presence until there had been so much damage that I could no longer ignore it.

Tom had daily frustrations with his boss. His boss always talked down to him and made him feel small. Tom had not had a raise in years, and yet the boss would give him so much to do that he would have to take work home at night. But Tom did not know when he was angry because he had built "The Wall," and he did not feel these moments of anger. His heart was filling up with bitterness, but he was not aware of it. After he would get home from work, his wife would do some little thing that irritated him, and he would explode with anger at her. She did not just receive Tom's reaction to what she just did, but she also received the entire load that had been building up inside Tom towards his boss. It was like an avalanche. One small disturbance was the trigger, and all the "snow" that had accumulated came surging down in one deluge and buried her.

Ski areas understand avalanches. They know that if they can keep the snow from accumulating on the mountain slopes above them they can prevent an avalanche. So they regularly set off small explosive charges in the snow to bring down small snow slides that are harmless. In this way they prevent huge buildups of snow that would inevitably come down in a devastating rush.

In the same way, Tom needed to listen to, and learn to recognize, every surge of anger that he felt. Then he could pray about it immediately and avoid the "accumulation" that would otherwise eventually (and inevitably) come out as outbursts of rage. If there is not

---

[43] "The Wall" I referred to on page 77.

an "accumulation" inside him, when people irritate him they only receive the reaction that relates to that single transgression, not his pent up reactions to all the other accumulated hurts inside him.

## We Are Needy

We are needy creatures. God made us that way. We need love, we need water, we need sleep, we need exercise, etc. There is nothing "selfish" about getting our legitimate needs met in a legitimate way. When our legitimate needs are not met, we are "hungry" and settle for meeting our needs in any way we can, perhaps including "illegitimate" ways, or groveling for whatever "crumbs" we can find.

For example, at this moment if I were to hand you a dirty, smelly glass of water, you would likely say, "No thank you," because you aren't that thirsty. However, if you had been wandering in the Sahara Desert for three days with no water, and then I offered you the dirty glass of water, you would eagerly snatch it from me and instantly consume it. Why? You would drink it because your need had become so great.

That is what happens when we consciously deny our legitimate needs (or perhaps are unaware of them because we have ignored them for so long). We become so empty inside that we are driven to accept inappropriate substitutes to stop the screams coming up from inside us.

## The "Code"

To appropriately end the turmoil of our negative emotions, we need to know how God intended for us to eliminate the pain, rather than to cover it up. He intended for us to eliminate the pain by addressing the cause of the pain. When we have a toothache, we can take a pain killer, or we can have the tooth fixed. When the tooth is "fixed," the pain stops.

Remember that emotional pain relates either to unmet psychological needs or to roots of sin that exist inside.

There are therefore two things we need to know about eliminating our emotional pain.

1. We need to listen to the pain rather than run from it. This way we can discover what it is telling us. For instance, when we are feeling lonely, our emotion is probably not telling us that we are angry with our boss for what he said today.

2. Then we need to address the cause of the pain by applying the appropriate "cure." Right now we need to seek out fellowship rather than forgive our boss. If we have judged our boss, forgiving him would be necessary; but that prayer would not cure our loneliness.

Unfortunately, nobody taught us how to do either of these, especially regarding the roots of sin. But it is possible to learn how to do both, and therefore, it is possible to eliminate the <u>cause</u> of our emotional pain so that the pain will stop.

## Understanding The Language Of Our Emotions

God gave us our "emotions," and He intended for them to be useful to us. It is therefore possible to learn this mysterious language that our Treasure Inside speaks to us. In later chapters I will go into more detail about learning this language, but here I want to point out a few important characteristics of our "emotions."

1. A negative emotion may be telling us of <u>an unmet appropriate emotional need,</u> such as the need for fellowship in the above example. If that need <u>is</u> met in an appropriate way, the negative emotion will go away and will likely be replaced by an emotion that feels good. We have received what we needed. For instance James, who is a little boy, needs a hug. The parent picks him up and holds him. The negative emotion will likely be replaced with a good

feeling of satisfaction, which tells James he is no longer needy. Now he is ready to be put down and again explore the world.

2. A negative emotion may be telling us about a root of sin that we <u>have just planted</u> inside, such as judging our boss in the above example. These events cause us the most difficulty, and are the most mysterious to us. If unresolved, such a root will cause problems in our life (See Chapter 3, "The Power of the Spirit Realm").

3. The emotional pain may <u>also</u> be telling us about an <u>older root</u> that we have not yet eliminated. For example, I may tend to feel lonely a lot because my parents never had time to spend with me. In this case the current event has touched this old root and triggered a response from it. It is like stubbing your toe. When you first injure it, there is pain. But until it heals, it seems as though you are constantly hitting it on something. Actually, you are probably not again hitting it hard enough to injure it further, but the toe is hyper-sensitive to pain. It is hyper-sensitive because of the previous injury. Therefore, one symptom of the presence of an old root deep inside us is when a small situation triggers a big response, a response that is out of proportion to what just happened. This is what happened to Tom in one of my previous examples. His previous Bitter Root Judgments accumulated and eventually he exploded in anger at his wife.

4. All negative "feelings," both physical and emotional, <u>are proportional</u> to the need. The more urgent or important, the more intense is the pain. If I have a slight discomfort in my tooth, I can take my time about getting it fixed. If the pain is intense, I need to get to the dentist immediately. I can't stand to wait! That is exactly why God designed feelings this way. The intense pain tells me there is a serious problem that needs immediate treatment, and the pain

motivates me to take action <u>now</u>. I find myself unable to postpone getting treatment.

5. The language of our "emotions" is not a language like English or Spanish. It is made up of little sensations which are specific to the nature of the hurt. I will ask clients how they feel about something; for instance, how their spouse treats them. Often the response is something like, "I feel as though he doesn't listen to me." This is not an emotion. This is an analysis. The emotion would be something like: "I feel abandoned, unimportant, demeaned, alone." If this concept is new to you, or if you are not used to naming your feelings, **see the end of Chapter 12** for a list of "feeling" words. You will find this list useful in helping you to describe what you are feeling at a given moment.

## Eliminating The Cause Of The Pain

Therefore, if there is a Bitter Root Judgment planted inside us, our negative emotions are our friend telling us about this problem. What do we do in response to the negative emotion (the "alarm" going off)? We need to key in the "code." When the cause of the alarm is sin, there is only one "code" that works. <u>The</u>

> **The most common source of emotional pain is the wound that sin plants in our heart.**

<u>"code" that God has provided is the provision for the washing away of our sin through the forgiveness provided by the sacrifice of Jesus</u>. This "code" works. When we forgive and are forgiven, the negative emotion stops. It stops because the wound that the pain was warning us about has been healed. The sin has been washed away, and Jesus has come into that place in our heart. The "burglar" is now gone. Jesus' provision truly is Good News!

When I was angry with the other driver who didn't go through the green light, I had judged him. I needed to take care of that as soon as I could,

> **When we forgive and are forgiven, the negative emotion stops.**

immediately if possible. That way I could catch the "burglar" before he had a chance to do any damage. After I pray, if I still find myself agitated, especially if my anger is extreme and is contaminating my day, I need to look for a long buried root of sin. Perhaps I had judged my parents for never paying attention to my needs. Even worse, perhaps I judged myself as being unworthy to have my needs met by others; and therefore it is left up to me to take care of myself. Certainly, it is true that the other driver was not sensitive to my needs, and it was his behavior that touched that wound deep inside me. But it wasn't what he did that was the problem. What planted the bitter root was <u>my reaction</u> to what he did. Feeling the negative emotion gives me an opportunity to know what happened, and thus I can pray and be set free from the consequences of the bitter root.

## It Is Complicated, And Yet Simple

The code to my home burglar alarm is simple, but this "code" to end my negative emotions appropriately is complex. It is complex because many of the old roots of bitterness are deeply buried and I have forgotten about them. I cannot remember many of them myself. It is therefore too complex for me to understand. But it is not too complicated for Jesus, and He will lead me in this process of finding the bitter roots and being healed. I may also need another person to walk through this with me, such as a trusted friend, or a counselor. I also need to listen to my Treasure Inside, who is telling me what is wrong inside.

Ideally, teaching me how to listen to my emotions and to then pray was the job assigned to my parents. In my own childhood, my parents were as ignorant about this as I, so there was no way for them to teach me. In fact, they did the opposite of facilitating my ability to hear my Treasure Inside **(See Chapter 9 for more on this part of you)** by giving me messages that emotions were

> **It is never too late to make friends with yourself.**

irrelevant. They wounded me and I built "The Wall," which reduced my innate ability to hear my emotions. Unfortunately, many parents are unable to mentor their children in order to help them hear what is going on in the Treasure Inside them. If this is true of you, now as an adult you need to have "The Wall" dismantled, and to learn what your parents should have taught you when you were very young --- how to understand the language of the valuable friend you have in your Treasure Inside. It is never too late to make friends with yourself.

When I first realized how shut down I had been inside, I questioned the Lord, "Why didn't I know this earlier?" I felt bitter because I had to suffer for many years before I became aware of the truth. But then I realized how blessed I was. Many people <u>never</u> learn about the "code," and they suffer for their whole life. We are blessed to know this now.

## Are "Bad" Emotions Sin?

Many of us have been taught that "bad" emotions are sin. For instance we may have been taught that it is a sin to feel jealous. However, it should now be clear to you that it is <u>not</u> a sin to feel jealous. There is nothing wrong with that emotion, and so we do not need to repent of feeling jealous. The emotion is simply the message system. There is a sin present, but <u>the sin is not the emotion</u>. There is a root of bitterness inside us (planted by a sinful reaction of judging), and we need to know about the presence of this bitter root.

85

- The judging was sin.
- The message (emotion) telling us this fact is <u>not</u> sin.


We <u>do</u> then need to find out what the root is and be healed of that. This may sound like hair splitting, but there is a profound difference between the <u>emotion</u> and the <u>root</u>. <u>The bitter root of sin exists, and the emotion is just the signal telling us about the root.</u> The signal is not sin, but rather it is just our faithful messenger, our helper, and our friend.

In ancient times, when a messenger brought bad news, the king had the messenger killed. Of course, the problem wasn't the messenger or the message he carried. The messenger was simply a mechanism for informing the king about something bad that was going on elsewhere. We now look at the king's response and see how ridiculous that is. And yet that is exactly what we have done if we have shut off our emotions because they are "bad."

## How The Sequence Works

Be aware that though the emotion itself is not sin, what I do in response to the emotion may be sin. For example, suppose someone insults me. I feel angry at them. The emotion is my friend, warning me that <u>I have already sinned</u> (I have judged the person, and thus planted a bitter root). Now I am at a decision point: I can hit the other person, and thus commit yet another additional sin; or I can forgive that person and remove the bitter root (sin) I have already planted. A third option would be for me to ignore the feeling, but then the bitter root will fester and grow and eventually produce more bad fruit.

## Repressing Emotions Hurts <u>Us</u>

Repressing or trying to squash our emotions produces negative consequences in our lives. We are the ones who suffer. When we repress the negative emotions to keep from feeling the pain, we miss out on the awareness that something inside needs attention. That is what the negative emotions are telling us. If we continue to ignore them, there will be unfortunate consequences. Whatever is wrong inside may eventually come to the surface in some fashion, because the problem inside will become too large to ignore. Ulcers, insomnia, and uncontrolled outbursts of anger are common examples of this. When we do not allow emotions to come "straight out" (listen to them and resolve them) as God intended, they eventually come out "sideways" and produce problems in our life. **See Chapter 10** on this war going on inside.

Since we are children of God, the Lord intends to transform us into His image. If we ignore the signals He sends up, our negative emotions do not have their intended purpose to guide us in our sanctification process. Thus we miss out on the transformation He wants us to experience.

## The Paradox Of "Selfishness"

Some people believe it is "selfish" to seek to have their own needs met. They believe that it is pleasing to God for them to <u>always</u> give up their own needs for the benefit of others, and so they believe it is a sin to seek to get their own needs met. This belief brings about a paradox.

1. When these people thus <u>try</u> to <u>always</u> give up their own needs, they become more needy inside, and thus more focused on getting their unmet needs met. When they ignore a need, the message from their Treasure Inside gets louder and louder and eventually becomes difficult to ignore. Thus they become highly motivated to fill their own need. They become more "selfish." To the degree they do <u>succeed</u> in denying their own need, they experience the unfortunate consequences which I have just listed ---- the emotion comes out "sideways."

2.  On the other hand, when they understand that they have legitimate needs, and now recognize that the message coming up from their Treasure Inside is their friend, they are able to get the need met in an appropriate way.  Because the need is not yet so severe that it is screaming at them for fulfillment, there is not an urgency about meeting the need.  They are then still in a position to be particular as to how the need is met.  They can thus succeed in having their legitimate need met in a legitimate way.  When their need is met, they are no longer focused on themselves and are free to give to others.  They become less "selfish."

Thus the paradox is that for those who try not to be "selfish," what seems so right (not being selfish) brings about failure.  What seems so wrong (getting their own needs met) would bring about success.  This seeming paradox is fueled by their neediness.  Unmet needs scream at them for fulfillment.  Met needs bring about peace inside, freedom, and the ability to love others as they love themselves.

## The Role Of Positive Emotions

God gave us both positive and negative emotions.  So far we have been focusing on the negative ones.  Remember, He made the negative ones unpleasant so we would <u>avoid</u> whatever was causing them.  The positive ones are also useful.  God made them pleasant so we would <u>approach</u> whatever causes them.  They signal the receipt of something good for us. When children need to be held, they hold up their hands so that their parent will pick them up and fill the need.  Once they have been filled with the touch of the parent, they are ready to get down and again explore the world.

Since we are needy creatures, it is important that we have a way of knowing what is good for us so we can seek it out and receive it. Feeling both positive and negative emotions is therefore meant to be our way of navigating through life.

Unfortunately, when we repress our negative feelings, we lose the good ones too. "The tragic thing about burying or smothering negative feelings is that it doesn't stop with them. The good, positive ones get clobbered at the same time." (Jacobs, p.25).

## Jesus Felt His Emotions

The Bible describes Jesus as experiencing many emotions. He was sad, He wept, He was angry, and He had compassion. [44] We are also instructed to experience emotions. [45] We are given permission to be angry, but we should not let it drive us into sinning. We are encouraged to be joyful. We are told that we can experience peace.

## Can You Rely On Your Emotions?

It may shock you to know that your emotions are always 100% accurate. Your emotions are not <u>sometimes</u> accurate, or <u>often</u> accurate. They are <u>always</u> accurate - - - <u>in one way</u>. They <u>always</u> tell you exactly what is going on <u>inside</u> you.

---

[44] **Matthew 9:36,** *but when He saw the multitudes, He was moved with compassion for them, because they were weary and scattered, like sheep having no shepherd.*

    **Mark 3: 5,** *So when He had looked around at them with anger, being grieved by the hardness of their hearts, He said to the man, "Stretch out your hand." And he stretched it out, and his hand was restored as whole as the other.*

    **Luke 19:41,** *Now as He drew near, He saw the city and wept over it,*

    **John 11:33; 38,** *Therefore, when Jesus saw her weeping, and the Jews who came with her weeping, He groaned in the spirit and was troubled. . . Then Jesus, again groaning in Himself, came to the tomb.*

    **John 11:35,** *Jesus wept.*

[45] **Matthew 5:4,** *"Blessed are those who mourn, For they shall be comforted."*

    **Romans 12:15,** *Rejoice with those who rejoice, and weep with those who weep.*

    **Romans 14:17,** *For the kingdom of God is not food and drink, but righteousness and peace and joy in the Holy Spirit.*

    **Ephesians 4:26,** *"Be angry, and do not sin." Do not let the sun go down on your wrath.*

    **Philippians 2:18,** *For the same reason you also be glad and rejoice with me.*

    **2 Timothy 1:4,** *greatly desiring to see you, being mindful of your tears, that I may be filled with joy,*

    **James 4:9,** *Lament and mourn and weep! Let your laughter be turned to mourning and your joy to gloom.*

Because of old wounds and the reactions that are triggered by their presence, our emotions <u>may</u> <u>not</u> be an accurate measure of what is going on <u>outside</u> of us. For instance, I might feel rejected by the host at a party,

> **Your emotions <u>always</u> tell you <u>exactly</u> what is going on <u>inside</u> you.**

only to find out later he liked me! My emotion was not an accurate indicator of what was happening in my relationship with the host at the party (what was happening <u>outside</u> me). Nevertheless, the feeling was giving me very important information about what was happening <u>inside</u> me. In this situation, my emotion was saying I have an old root of bitterness that was triggered when I felt rejected. I need to know this so that I can find the old root of rejection and be healed.

<u>Whenever</u> my emotion is not appropriate to the circumstances, this is an <u>important clue</u> that there is a wound inside me that needs to be taken care of. In these situations I might blame others, or circumstances, or dismiss my emotion as undesirable. And sometimes "The Wall" is so impenetrable that I may not feel some emotions at all; or the feeling vanishes in a flash, before I can recognize it.

Whenever and however I dismiss my emotion, I rob myself of the opportunity of seeing that I have a wound inside me. Then I miss out on the opportunity of being healed. My emotion was my friend giving me important information about what was going on inside me.

## A Strange Language

If you have not been listening to what your emotions are telling you, their "language" will likely be strange to you. Our parents were supposed to teach us how to understand this language. If they didn't (and mine sure didn't, because they didn't know it themselves), and if we have been running from our emotions, we are probably not very adept at describing how we feel. Saying, "I feel like he doesn't listen to me" is not a feeling. It is a conclusion. Saying "I feel unimportant," or "I feel lonely," are descriptions of emotions. If you have difficulty describing what you are feeling, the list of negative and positive emotions at the end of **Chapter 12** may help you put a name to what you are feeling. We need to learn this language so that we can understand what our emotions are telling us, thereby benefiting from the information.

## A Subtle Trap

Many times Christians harbor bitterness towards someone, and explain that it is "righteous anger." There is no such thing in a human being as "righteous anger." Jesus got angry and threw the money changers out of the temple, but He gets to do that. He is God. We aren't.

> *Be angry, and do not sin, do not let the sun go down on your wrath, nor give place to the devil* (Ephesians 4:26-27).

This is a recognition that we will get angry. But if we don't apply the blood of Jesus to the bitter root (forgive and be forgiven), the enemy has a foothold to impel us into sinful behavior. The "bad root" that was planted will be used by the devil to produce "bad fruit." This New Testament verse is a shortened version of an Old Testament saying:

> *Be angry, and do not sin. Meditate within your heart on your bed, and be still. Offer the sacrifices of righteousness, and put your trust in the Lord* (Psalm 4:4-5).

When we get angry, we need to take the time to pay attention to what just happened, and apply the blood of Jesus. We have that pathway to righteousness available to us; but David, who wrote this psalm, did not have that available to him.

Since Jesus did provide the way of sanctification, He is very eager to guide us in this process. He knows that we need to be told about the presence of a root of sin, so **He utilizes this communication system** to alert us to any bitter roots that

**Jesus uses our emotions to guide our sanctification.**

we have planted. Since we sin frequently, this means that we have the opportunity to frequently be in touch with Jesus. And as we practice listening, in this way we become more and more adept at hearing His voice.

# Chapter 8

# The Bad Part Of You
## *Your God-wannabe*

*For I know that in me (that is, in my flesh) nothing good dwells;*
*for to will is present with me, but how to perform what is good I*
*do not find*  (Romans 7:18).

This scripture makes it clear that the "bad" part of me can be termed my "flesh."  When the Bible uses the term "flesh," most of us immediately jump to the conclusion that what is being referred to is our entire self, and it is "bad."  We think that "flesh" always causes us to be engaged in sinful behavior, such as fornication, drunkenness, or idolatry (Galatians 5:19-21).

However, it may surprise you to know that when the Bible uses the term "flesh," it is not always talking about a "bad" thing.  For example, when the Bible said that Jesus came in the flesh, did He come in something that was "bad?"  Since He was sinless, He couldn't possibly be a part of something that was sinful. [46]

*Every spirit that confesses that Jesus Christ has come in the flesh*
*is of God, and every spirit that does not confess that Jesus Christ*
*has come in the flesh is not of God.* (1 John 4:2-3).

---

[46] **Romans 1:3,** *Concerning His Son Jesus Christ our Lord, who was born of the seed of David according to the flesh.*

**1 Peter 3:18,** *For Christ also suffered once for sins, the just for the unjust, that He might bring us to God, being put to death in the flesh but made alive by the Spirit.*

**1 Peter 4:1,** *Therefore, since Christ suffered for us in the flesh, arm yourselves also with the same mind, for he who has suffered in the flesh has ceased from sin.*

**2 John 1:7,** *For many deceivers have gone out into the world who do not confess Jesus Christ as coming in the flesh.  This is a deceiver and an antichrist.*

The Lord also spoke to the people of Israel and said,

> *Then I will give them one heart, and I will put a new spirit within them, and take the stony heart out of their flesh, and give them a heart of flesh* (Ezekiel 11:19).

It is evident from the context that the "heart of flesh" that the Lord was going to give them is a good thing, not a bad thing.

## When "Flesh" Is Not Bad

In fact, there are several ways that "flesh" (the Greek word *sarx*) in the Bible refers to something that is not "bad." What follows are primarily New Testament references, which were written in Greek.

1. Flesh can refer to our entire person.
2. Flesh can refer to the physical part of man.
3. Flesh can refer to our creatureliness and frailty, the fact that we are finite and vulnerable.
4. Flesh can refer to something that is purely natural or external. [47]

## "Fuzzy" Words

In our Western world we like to think our words are precise tools which we can use to understand perfectly what someone else is saying. We tend to transfer this concept to the Bible and to the languages in which it

---

[47] Rudolf Bultmann adds to the variety of the meanings of *sarx*: "In fact, like *psyche* and *pneuma* . . . *sarx* can even be used to designate the person himself" (p. 233). And, "Thus, *sarx* can mean the whole sphere of that which is earthly or natural . . . Or, differently said, 'to live' or 'to walk in the flesh' means nothing else than simply 'to lead one's life as a man,' an idea which in itself does not involve any ethical or theological judgment but simply takes note of a fact; not a norm but a field or a sphere is indicated by 'in the flesh" (Bultmann, <u>Theology of the New Testament</u>, Part II, pp.234, 235-236).

was written. With accurate definitions we can clearly understand Scripture. But often words are not so precise.

Have you ever wondered why biologists, anthropologists, and other scientists use such long words to specify a certain species (for instance, "*saintpaulia ionantha*" for "African violet")? They do this so that when they talk with other scientists, they know <u>exactly</u> what species is being discussed. They do this because many English words have numerous meanings, some meanings of a given word being unrelated to each other.

For instance, the English noun "round" has several possible meanings. When hunting, or on the firing range, it refers to one thing (a bullet). When in a bar drinking, it refers to something else (drinks for everyone). It would be a good idea if the bartender did not confuse these two meanings when you ask for a "round." Otherwise it might hurt a lot.

Many of the important concepts in the Bible are explained using fuzzy words (since that was all that was available to the writers). Then how can we understand what the author is telling us? We can gain an accurate understanding by paying attention to the "context," to what the writer is talking about at the moment. The bartender needs to recognize that the person wants to buy drinks. The manager of the firing range needs to recognize that the person wants some ammunition.

*Sarx* (the Greek word for "flesh") is one of those fuzzy words. It is unfortunate and confusing that the word "flesh" has such a wide range of meanings. But with careful study of the context of various biblical passages in which the word is used, we can better understand what the writer is trying to say. We always must be on guard so that we do not apply the wrong meaning in a given context or situation.

# The Bad Part

In the New Testament sometimes the term "flesh" does not mean something bad, but in other passages it <u>does</u> mean a bad thing in us. When "flesh" is referring to the "Bad Part," it can be referring to one of three possibilities.

---

**When "flesh" <u>is</u> referring to the "Bad Part," it can be referring to one of three possibilities:**

1. **Sensuality or lawlessness. Here it means a disregard for God's moral standards.**
2. **<u>Trying</u> hard to be good!**
3. **Our tendency to respond to perceived wounding with bitterness, judgment, and blame.**

---

It may be a surprise to you that to try to be good by your own willpower is not just futile, it is in fact sinful. The tendency to do this comes out of your "flesh" – the "Bad Part." [48]

---

[48] In Jesus' day the Pharisees were not trying to be bad (# 1 in the box above), but they were trying to be good (# 2 above). They were trying diligently (with their own willpower) to obey the Law. Yet Jesus told them they were of their father the Devil (John 8:44), and they were white washed tombs full of dead men's bones (Matthew 23:27-28). In other words, Jesus said they were not only failing to keep the Law, but they were full of sin in trying to do so.

The Pharisees were under the delusion that they had in themselves the strength to obey the Law. As we have seen, this is a subtle but profound way of taking God's place. When we are reaping from the operation of God's law, we are in fact impotent (see Chapter 3). To think that we have the power to stop this reaping is demeaning to God. If we could do it ourselves, Christ died in vain.

## The Common Denominator

Behind all three of these tendencies of the Bad Part is a common theme. All of these tendencies are based upon a "self-reliant attitude of the man who puts his trust in his own strength and in that which is controllable by him." [49] There is something in us, in our "flesh," which wants to be God. This is what happened in the Garden of Eden: Satan told Eve, *"For God knows that in the day you eat of it your eyes will be opened, and you will be like God"* (Genesis 3:5). Eve and Adam believed Satan and ate of the fruit. From that moment on, we humans have had the tendency to want to be our own god. That is the dynamic behind the "Bad Part" of each of us, which is one of the uses of the word "flesh."

> **For me to try to be good by my own willpower is not just futile, it is in fact sinful; and the tendency to do this comes out of my "flesh" – the "Bad Part."**

## The Primal Sin

This desire to take God's place, to be our own god, is foundational to our difficulties in this life. This desire and drive is therefore the "Primal Sin"---the bedrock of our sinful side.

> "For just this is the essence of flesh: the essence of the man who understands himself in terms of himself, who wants to secure his own existence . . . This then is sin: rebellion against God, forgetting that man is a creature, misunderstanding oneself and putting oneself in God's place" (Bultmann, Existence and Faith, p.81).

---

[49] Bultmann, Theology of the New Testament, Part II, p.240.

"But man misunderstands himself and puts himself in the place of God. And every man comes out of a history that is governed by this misunderstanding. He comes out of a lie; he is determined by the flesh whose power he cannot break. Were he to imagine that he could break it, he would assume that he does have himself in his own power after all and would thereby repeat the primal sin" (Bultmann, Theology of the New Testament, Part I, p.83). [50]

> **I need to have the blood of Jesus ever available to me, so that He can clean up the mess that my God-wannabe keeps making inside me.**

## Don't "Throw The Baby Out With The Bathwater"

When we judge ourselves, or try to "die to self," it is because we have come to see everything hidden inside us as "bad." Everything seems to be in one "container." Since pain and the impulse to bad behavior come from someplace "inside," we conclude that everything "inside" is "bad."

When we see everything below our level of consciousness as "bad", we seek to distance ourselves from all of it. Essentially, we build "The Wall" between our conscious self and our subconscious self.

---

[50] "The primal sin is not an inferior morality, but rather the understanding of oneself in terms of oneself and the attempt to secure one's own existence by means of what one himself establishes, by means of one's own accomplishments " (Bultmann, Existence & Faith, p.81).

"And since all pursuit, even the perverted sort, is, in intention, pursuit of life, this means seeking life where it is not - in the created world. For to deny God as Creator is to turn away from Him to the creation . . . Hence, the ultimate sin reveals itself to be the false assumption of receiving life not as the gift of the Creator but procuring it by one's own power, of living from one's self rather than from God" (Bultmann, Theology of the New Testament, Part II, p.232).

However, below our level of consciousness there are at least three areas, which are symbolized by the containers in the diagram that follows.

The diagram on the next page is an over-simplification of what we are like inside, presented to help you understand that everything inside us is not the "Bad Part." There is much more. Because Scripture is not precise about it, I cannot be dogmatic about everything that is inside each of these "containers," nor that there are only three "containers" hidden inside. But I can with the backing of Scripture say that there is a Good Part, there is a Bad Part, and these two parts do not constitute all there is. I can also infer that there is a part somewhere inside that contains good roots and bad roots. We are incredibly complex inside, and the Lord is the only one who knows the whole picture. What is most important is to know that there is both a "Bad Part" and a "Good Part" inside us.

## There Are Multiple Places Inside Us

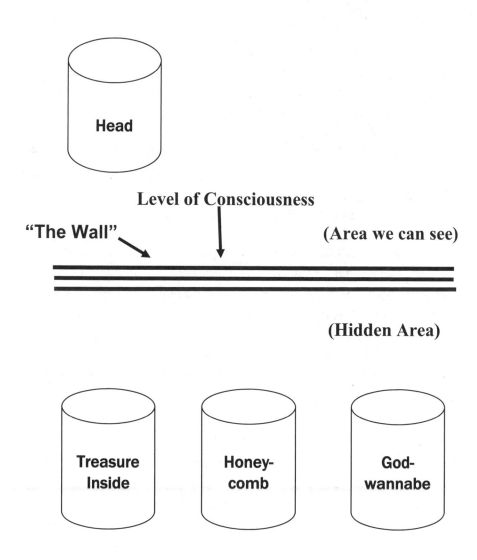

When we judge ourselves, we confuse the Treasure Inside (the "Good Part" (See **Chapter 9** for details of the image of God in us) with the God-wannabe ("Bad Part," see **Chapter 8** for details) and with the Bitter Roots (the black places in the "Honeycomb," **Chapter 4**). We lump all these together. We therefore condemn <u>everything</u> hidden inside us. We literally "throw the baby out with the bath water." The "Good Part" (the image of God in us that is innocent) gets condemned along with the part(s) that are guilty.

Understanding that there are several parts hidden in us will facilitate treating each part appropriately. Our Treasure Inside and God-wannabe (Flesh) can't be changed (or "healed"). They will always be what they were from the moment that Adam and Eve fell.

On the other hand, the "Honeycomb" (discussed in **Chapter 4**) can be healed. It is in a sense the "battle ground" where darkness and light compete. When, because of the influence of our God-wannabe, we judge, a Bitter Root is planted in our Honeycomb.

However, this damage can be repaired by forgiving and being forgiven by Jesus. The Bitter Root can thus be changed into a good root through the blood of Jesus. Then light wins over darkness. Then the new good root will produce good fruit.

Finally, the image of God in us needs to be affirmed and loved. Love is the "fuel" that our Treasure Inside runs on. This is why it is so devastating to judge and to hate that part.

## Where Does "Die To Self" Fit In?

There is a perspective that says that we should "die to self." This view, while not uncommon in churches, often has destructive results. Many who advocate and teach this perspective often correctly say there is a part of us that does need to die and be reborn in the likeness of Jesus. However, the destruction in "die to self" comes about through a misunderstanding of what is meant by "self." These students get the impression this means that <u>everything inside</u> them is bad and needs to "die." In other words, in the previous diagram everything below the "Level of Consciousness" needs to "die."

When this misunderstanding exists, though they are believers in Jesus, these students are prone to feel defeated. They develop a deep distrust of everything inside them - they "throw out the baby with the bathwater." Their Treasure Inside does not need to be obliterated, because he or she is made in the image of God (and therefore thrives on love). In fact, being a part of the person's essence, it is impossible to eliminate the Treasure Inside. These believers are wounded and miserable because they are doing exactly the opposite of what they need to do - they are hating rather than loving their Treasure Inside (Matthew 22:39). Because their Treasure Inside is real, he or she continues to "speak" to them by sending up pain. Thus they attempt to suppress <u>all</u> that is inside.

## Creating An Insolvable Dilemma

To the degree that they succeed in building "The Wall" to shut off their non-conscious self, they experience all the problems that "The Wall" creates. To the degree they do not succeed, they feel guilty and condemned. It is an insolvable dilemma, because either way they lose. They become miserable and defeated.

As I have previously shown, when we attempt to gain an understanding of biblical principles, a great deal of what we struggle with is based upon a misunderstanding of what a particular word means. These misperceptions are understandable for a couple of reasons. Since so many of the theological words we use have such broad ranges of meaning, how do we know which meaning applies in a particular passage? And there are always difficulties in translating from Greek to English. In addition, our popular culture and the New Age have redefined some words that would otherwise be useful. In order to avoid such a tragic misunderstanding, I would recommend not using the phrase "die to self." It would be much more accurate and fruitful to speak about

Jesus pulling out the bitter roots and replacing them with His presence inside. [51]

## Pride

In much of the church, one of the greatest sins that one is to avoid committing is the sin of pride. In this case, the use the term "pride" is meant to describe the human tendency to want to be our own God. I think this is misleading, or perhaps even dangerous, because the word "pride" is then usually understood to mean "I am really something great." [52] Therefore, to eliminate "pride" means to come to the place where "I am nothing." Consequently, to label a person's flaw as "pride" is to put him or her on a quest to see themselves as "nothing." As I have just been discussing, people are not "nothing." They are made in the image of God. Seeing themselves as "nothing" aggravates the already present low esteem of self that most people have, and perhaps paradoxically brings about building of "The Wall," and further wounding and destruction inside. Ironically, seeing themselves as nothing will likely impel people into arrogant behavior, as a means of not feeling like a worm. Most braggarts are like this.

Arrogant behavior (or "pride") <u>is a sin,</u> [53] whereas the "Bad Part" I have just described is <u>our sin-nature,</u> our God-wannabe. The sin of

---

[51] "Die to self" appears nowhere in the New Testament, and is in fact contrary to the clear teachings of the Bible.

[52] Webster's Dictionary defines "proud," in part, as "having or displaying excessive self-esteem." The word "pride" is, in part, defined as "the quality or state of being proud: inordinate self-esteem."

[53] It is interesting that the term "pride" is very rare in the New Testament. It only appears three times (Strong's, p.840). Apparently the New Testament writers did not see it as a major issue to be addressed. In light of this low emphasis, it is interesting how much emphasis the Western church has placed on the need to not be "proud." In contrast to this, sexual sins like "fornication" and "adultery" are addressed dozens of times in the New Testament.

"pride" can be repented of and washed in the blood of Jesus. [54] Then it is gone. It no longer exists as far as God is concerned. On the other hand, what I have described as our God-wannabe is not "pride." It is something much deeper, and it has nothing whatsoever to do with how we feel about ourselves. It is a part of our very nature as a result of the fall, and it is in every human being. There is nothing we can do to remove it. It will be present as long as we live on this earth; and it is present in people whose "self-esteem" is practically zero.

## Legalism

Legalism is deadly. Legalism is the process of trying to please God by keeping His rules, by trying to live a holy life through our willpower. However, if our "bad behavior" is bad fruit from a bad root, attempting to keep the rules is worse than futile. It is sin. Our God-wannabe will impel us to try to do it ourselves. Therefore, when we are told what we are supposed to do without being taught HOW the blood of Jesus can change us inside, we are actually being encouraged to sin! It is because of this deadly trap that Jesus was so hard on the scribes and Pharisees.

## Summary

The word "flesh" in the New Testament refers to a wide range of things, many of which are not "bad." However, one use of the word "flesh" does refer to the place inside us which does not trust God, and which wants to take His place. It is out of this fallen place that most (if not all) of our tendency to sin arises. It manifests itself in disregard of God's commandments, in zeal to obey Him out of our own strength (our willpower), and in our tendency to take His place by judging.

When we are children, we don't understand that we are multifaceted inside. Therefore, when we discover that we sometimes

---

[54] **Isaiah 43:25,** "*I, even I, am He who blots out your transgressions for My own sake; and I will not remember your sins.*"

    **Jeremiah 31:34b,** "*For I will forgive their iniquity, and their sin I will remember no more.*"

tend to be "bad," we then judge <u>everything</u> hidden inside us as "bad." We then "throw the baby out with the bathwater." This is tragic, because there is a "good" place inside us that needs to be loved. Not being able to love that "good" place brings about destruction in our lives.

When we understand the truth that we are multifaceted inside, that there are "good," "bad," and "wounded" places inside us, we are in a position to begin to successfully walk out our healing.

> *"And you shall know the truth, and the truth shall make you free . . . Therefore if the Son makes you free, you shall be free indeed"* (John 8:32, 36).

# Chapter 9

## The Good Part Of You

### *You Are Not All Bad*

In the deep recesses of your being, how do you <u>feel</u> about yourself? I am not talking about your accomplishments or the image you present to the world, but how you feel deep down inside about yourself. For instance,

- Do you tend to see others as better and more capable than you?
- Do you always feel "less than" others?
- Do others seem to you to be more worthy of happiness and prosperity?
- Do you have a "poverty mentality?" (A poverty mentality is the expectation that you will never have more than the minimum necessary to live on, and that you are not worthy of more).
- Are you too easily embarrassed?
- Are you petrified to speak in front of a group?
- Do you live in fear of being rejected?
- Do you often feel like a worm?

It may surprise you to know that most of us would answer "yes" to many of these questions! Most assuredly, I was one of them.

Why would you feel this way? Is there nothing good that dwells in you? Do you therefore need to "die to self?" After all, if you are "bad," this would explain why you feel like a worm.

## Who Does God Say We Are?

God doesn't agree with this view we may have of ourselves. He is very clear about this. <u>We are made in His image.</u> You are. I am. It is not just God in us that is good (though there are also places like that). There are places in each of us that are purely "us," that are a part of who we are, that are good. It is not just the Holy Spirit in us that is good. When God said, *"Let Us make man in Our image, according to Our likeness"* (Genesis 1:26),[55] He did not say, "Let Us make man to <u>be Us</u>." We are separate creatures from Him. We are unique, but made in His image. He is the pattern, but we are

> **You are not a worm. You are made in the image of God, and that Good Part of you still exists inside you.**

not Him, and He is not us.[56] This reality may be difficult for many to grasp, since there has been so much teaching and preaching about how awful we are.

## His Image Did Not Leave Us When Adam And Eve Sinned

We are made in His image,[57] and His image still dwells in us.[58] Theologians do not disagree regarding the fact that the image of God dwells in us <u>now</u>. Where there is dispute is in regard to exactly what

---

[55] When speaking of "Us" in this passage, God is referring to the Holy Trinity.

[56] Some say that our spirit is the "good part," but that view does not match Scripture.

[57] Genesis 1:26-27 says the following: *Then God said, "Let us make man in our image, according to our likeness; let them have dominion over the fish of the sea"* . . . *So God created man in His own image, in the image of God He created him; male and female He created them.*

[58] One might be tempted to say here that the image of God was in man before the fall, but after the fall, we were totally corrupted. However, Genesis 9:6, speaking after the fall, says: *Who ever sheds man's blood, by man his blood shall be shed; for in the image of God He made man.* So it is evident that the image of God still resided in man after the fall.

James 3:9 says the following, referring to the tongue: *With it we bless our God and father, and with it we curse men, who have been made in the image of God.* So, the image of God still resided in people in the time of James.

constitutes the Good Part and what makes up the Bad Part. This dispute is not likely to be resolved until Jesus comes again, because the Scripture is not specific enough to tell us. Fortunately, we don't need to know in detail, because Jesus knows. The key point for us to realize is that <u>there is, here and now, a good part in each of us that is made in the image of God!</u> [59]

## Humility And Pride

Humility is a word that is frequently misused. Often humility is viewed as recognizing what a worm I am, and how bad I am. "I am just an old sinner." But humility really means to <u>see myself the way God sees me</u>. When Jesus walked the earth He was humble, and yet He did not see Himself as a worm. He did not see Himself as less than He was, nor more than He was. He saw Himself as God the Father saw Him. He was the only begotten Son and He was God, but He was not God the Father. He did the will of the Father, not His own will (Matthew 26:39), because God the Father was preeminent.

Humility is about truth. We are not to see ourselves as more than we are, nor less than we are. Certainly, to see the truth about who we are in comparison with who God is eliminates the possibility of prideful boasting on our part. And yet, we are valuable because we are valuable

---

[59] This "good part" is what I am calling the Treasure Inside, and it is the core of our being. It is a gift from God, and it can't be changed. Everybody who has children knows that each child was born with certain gifts and propensities. Children are not simply raw material to be shaped into any form we choose. If they sense that they are unacceptable to us, they will try to change in order to please us. Because their Treasure Inside can't be changed, they will fail in their attempt to become acceptable, and they will begin to see themselves as fatally flawed.

**Psalm 139:13-14:** *For You have formed my inward parts; You have covered me in my mother's womb. I will praise You, for I am fearfully and wonderfully made; marvelous are Your works, and that my soul knows very well. My frame was not hidden from You, when I was made in secret, and skillfully wrought in the lowest parts of the earth.* This is hardly the description of a creature that is "all bad."

to God.[60]  At the same time, it is important that we find out who the unique person is that God made us to be.  To recognize our strengths that He gave us as a gift is not prideful or wrong.  Pride says that we did something to earn it.  Gifts by their very nature are not earned.  They are freely bestowed on us and are dependent on the giver, not the receiver.  So our strengths are free gifts bestowed on us, not things we manufactured or earned by our own effort.[61]  Pride is to see myself as more than I am.  See **Chapter** 8, "The Bad Part Of You," for more on pride.

## Why Do We See Ourselves As Worms?

Let me try to explain why so many of us feel badly about ourselves.  For some of us, we got constant messages from our parents that we weren't worth much.  Most importantly, our parents did not give us messages that confirm the truth about our worth and our Treasure Inside.

## Other Voices

Our siblings likely also gave us these same messages that did not confirm our worth.  Since they were raised in the same home, they also suffered from Type A Trauma.  In such a home there is competition for the few crumbs of

> **The voices that wounded us are:**
>
> 1. **Parents**
> 2. **Siblings**
> 3. **Our culture**
> 4. **The church**

---

[60] **Romans 5:8:** *But God demonstrates His own love toward us, in that while we were still sinners, Christ died for us.*  See also Ephesians 2:4, 2 Thessalonians 2:16, 1 John 4:10.

[61] "Today I understand vocation" (what I do) "quite differently - not as a goal to be achieved but as a gift to be received.  Discovering vocation does not mean scrambling toward some prize just beyond my reach but accepting the treasure of true self I already possess.  Vocation does not come from a voice 'out there' calling me to become something I am not.  It comes from a voice 'in here' calling me to be the person I was born to be, to fulfill the original selfhood given me at birth by God" (Palmer, p.10).

The Blessing which are available in the family. Each child is trying to raise himself above the others, because if he can feel superior to another child, he won't feel so badly about himself at that moment.

I have an older sister who was also very wounded by Type A Trauma. She was three years older than I, was a brilliant student, and was much larger than I was. When I was growing up she would set traps for me and play tricks on me to prove how much better she was, and she used to beat me up and take my stuff. She used to make fun of me, and called me "Shrimpo," because for much of our time growing up I only came up to her shoulder. She did all of these things to make herself feel a little better about herself, and what she said and did tore me down even further. Her message just added to my already fragile self-image.

Our culture also tells us how unworthy we are. The other children are doing the same thing as our siblings – competing for the crumbs of blessing that are available. Our culture is obsessed with being Number One, and competing to be Number One is seen as a wonderful thing! Since by definition there can only be one Number One, that makes the rest of us "losers." And those who are Number One in football are probably not Number One in math, or art, or perhaps anything except athletics. Thus they too are "losers." Therefore we are all losers, and most of us feel that way about ourselves. It is a cultural sickness, and is beautifully described as such by Alfie Kohn in his book, No Contest.[62]

Interestingly, when we compare ourselves with others, the areas where we aren't as good as the others are what impact us. Ironically, when we become Number One at something, it seems hollow. The good feeling of having achieved this victory is fleeting, and we still feel badly about ourselves, because we focus on those areas where we fall short. God is clear about this: *But they, measuring themselves by themselves, and comparing themselves among themselves, are not wise* (2 Corinthians 10:12, KJV).

---

[62] Kohn, Alfie, in bibliography.

The Church has also tended to focus on the bad, giving us the impression that there is nothing good that dwells in us.

One scripture presented in support of this is Romans 7:18: *For I know that in me (that is in my flesh) nothing good dwells.* It is in my flesh <u>only</u> that nothing good dwells, and these teachers assume this refers to all of my natural being. But flesh (Greek *sarx*) is another fuzzy Greek word. A detailed study reveals that my flesh, as referred to in this scripture, is only a part of me, not all of my being. Read Chapter 8, "The Bad Part Of You" for more on this. Jeremiah Chapter 17 is often raised as proof that nothing good dwells in me. Again, we are faced with a fuzzy word, the Hebrew word *leb*. There is significant doubt that Jeremiah is referring to our entire inner man.[63]

Further evidence we see of our own awfulness is that we are not living up to the standards laid out for us by the church. Deep inside we

---

[63] **Jeremiah, Chapter 17** says in part, *The heart of man is deceitful above all things and desperately wicked; who can know it?* As I have said earlier, we really can't specify that it's my heart where the wickedness lies. I cannot say with biblical authority exactly what part of me is deceitful and desperately wicked, because the Hebrew word here translated into English as "heart" is translated as many inner parts of me in other parts of the Old Testament. It is the translators' choice to use "heart," but there are several other options. Therefore the best I can really say in translating this verse in Jeremiah is something more like, "Somewhere deep inside of man there is a place that is deceitful above things and desperately wicked; who can know it?" Going beyond this is speculative.

Likewise, I can also only say that somewhere deep inside me there is a part of me that is made in the image of God. When faced with such doubt about the exact meaning of a word, we need to rely on other areas of the Word of God to clarify the meaning, if that is indeed possible. Some issues mentioned in the Bible will always remain fuzzy.

Further evidence that Jeremiah 17 is not referring to my Treasure Inside is the destruction that occurs in my life when I see myself as all bad. Admittedly this is only indirect scriptural evidence, but it is very powerful evidence; because it is true that whenever I align myself with God's truth, blessings flow. When I align myself with a lie, curses occur. This is simply the way God's laws work.

know we are falling short, and we feel that others are more successful as Christians. I then think, "I am surely bad." [64]

So we believed all these voices that surrounded our formative years. Certainly, we think, they can't all be wrong. From all of this we receive our identity. We see ourselves as bad.

But these voices are all wrong. God sees us differently, and He is always right.

## How Can We See Ourselves As God Sees Us?

Many other teachers and authors have made lists of scriptures that tell us how much God loves us, how valuable we are in His sight, how we are His children, etc. They encourage us to meditate on this list, with the implication that this exercise will convince us of who we really are. While it is very important to know how God feels about us, meditating on such a list (with our head) will not change how we feel about ourselves. Those of you that have tried this know how ineffective, frustrating, and discouraging this is. In our head we know how God see us, but the messages fail to make the journey to our heart. Our feelings don't change.

Then how can you change how you feel about yourself? That is what this book is intended to show you. If you read the book and walk it out, you will begin to see yourself as God sees you, because the living God will show you. As you begin to feel His love, the lies about how bad you are will be washed away.

---

[64] In many Christian circles, and indeed in our culture itself, there is a subtle but profound distrust of everything that comes up from inside us. Therefore, we attempt to consciously monitor and control our behavior with our intellect and willpower. Whenever we do this we are falling into the trap of striving, and are doomed to fail. Instead, we need to recognize there is a good part inside us that is our friend, learn to discern his or her voice, and follow that leading. Indeed, there is also a "bad part" inside us (read Chapter 8), but that voice is very different than the voice of our Treasure Inside (read Chapter 9)..

God communes with our Treasure Inside. See the diagram on the next page. When we are friends with our Treasure Inside, and the wall dissipates, we are enabled to have fellowship with the Lord.

## Summary

The purpose of this chapter has been to help you recognize some misconceptions about how bad you are.

There is a part of you that was corrupted by The Fall, but this corrupted part is not <u>all</u> of who you are. There is a part of you that is made in the image of God. It is "you," it is good, and it still exists in

> **For you to be sanctified, all that is "you" does not have to die. You are not rotten to the core.**

you. God says so in His Word. This is true whether you believe it or not.

A key part of your sanctification process (Inner Healing) is a complete change of attitude towards who you are. There is buried treasure inside you. You need to come to know that this is true before you can possibly be reconciled with yourself and have harmony inside. After all, who would want to love and be best friends with something evil?

For you to be sanctified (changed into the image of Jesus), all that is "you" does not have to die. You are not rotten to the core. God does not intend to annihilate you and replace you with Jesus. The real "you," your "Treasure Inside," is already made in God's image - and thus does not need to be sanctified further.

However, your "Honeycomb" (**Chapter 4**) does contain areas that are not holy, and which do need to be transformed. And there is a part of you that is your fallen nature, (*sarx*, your "God-wannabe").

# Chapter 10

# There Is A War Going On

It would be helpful if I could directly observe the presence of a "bad root" inside me. After all, if I observe that my hair needs combing, I can then comb it. If I see that my hands are dirty, I can wash them. Unfortunately, we cannot directly observe a "bad root." It resides below our level of consciousness.

For some reason, the Lord created us with both a "Conscious Self," and a "Non-conscious Self." The diagram below is offered to help to make this clear:

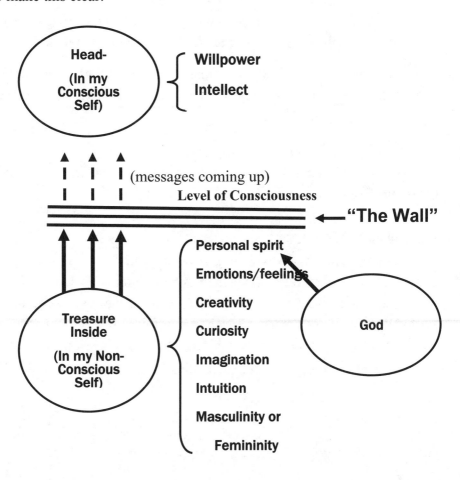

What I am calling our "Treasure Inside" is the part of us that is made in the image of God. <u>We are made in His image</u>. You are. I am. It is not just God in us that is good (though there are also places like that). There are places in each of us that are purely "us," that are a part of who we are, that are good. It is not just the Holy Spirit in us that is good. When God said, *"Let Us make man in Our image, according to Our likeness"* (Genesis 1:26). He did not say, "Let Us make man to <u>be Us</u>." We are separate creatures from Him. We are unique, but made in His image. He is the pattern, but we are not Him, and He is not us. This reality may be difficult for many to grasp, since there has been so much teaching and preaching about how awful we are. It is this image of God in us that I am calling our **"Treasure Inside." See Chapter 9.**

> **Your "Treasure Inside" exists, and is made in the image of God!**

Scripture is clear that our "Treasure Inside" exists. What I have listed are some of the attributes that God placed in there, though there are undoubtedly more. [65]

In this diagram I am not implying that our personal spirit is God. However, for Christians it is true that God does dwell in our Non-conscious Self.

## How We Can Perceive

We cannot directly observe what is going on below our level of consciousness. Our "Treasure Inside" is in our Non-conscious Self, and he or she observes what is going on in there. God installed a signal system whereby our "Treasure Inside" can inform our Conscious Self of what is occurring below our level of consciousness. That signal system is made up of our emotions and other subtle senses and awarenesses. [66]

---

[65] For more on your "Treasure Inside," also **see Chapter 9.**

[66] This is a very robust signal system, with many facets. A few examples are: emotions, intuition, creativity, empathy, dreams, visions, the voice of God.

Our cars have "oil lights" on the dashboard. That has been provided so that we can know about the oil level in the engine without us having to directly look into the oil pan. There is a sensor in the engine that observes that oil level. If the oil level gets below a certain point, the sensor sends a signal to the "oil light" to turn on, so that we can know the oil is low. It is a way that the car says "ouch." Then we can pull over to the side of the road and add some oil.

There are several other things that are also important for us to know about the status of the car. Therefore there is also a temperature gauge, a battery light, a "handbrake on" light, a "door open" light, etc. Each is necessary to give us specific important information.

Likewise, the messages that our "Treasure Inside" sends up to our Conscious Self are also specific to an important condition going on below our Level of Consciousness. That way we can consciously do the appropriate thing to fix the situation.

If we ignore the "oil light" in our car, something really bad is eventually going to happen to the engine. When the engine freezes up, we will be able to consciously and directly know that the engine had needed oil

Pilots who fly in the dark or in clouds need to trust their instruments. Their instruments give them information that they would otherwise have no way of knowing. When they cannot actually see the horizon with their naked eye, their own other physical senses can fool them. If they don't trust their instruments, lots of bad things can happen - such as going around in circles or crashing into the ground. Because it is so important that they trust their instruments, pilots have to go through extensive training so that they understand what the instruments are telling them, and to trust them.

My "Treasure Inside" is my friend, who knows what is going on below my level of consciousness. In conjunction with the Holy Spirit Who dwells inside me, I am told about it. I need to learn what those

> **My "Treasure Inside" is my friend who tells me what is going on in my Non-conscious Self.**

messages are saying, <u>and to trust them</u>; because it is always important information. If I don't listen to them or trust them and take corrective action, bad things can end up happening; because there is a war going on below my level of consciousness.

## There Is A War Going On

Unfortunately, below my level of consciousness there is residing another entity besides my "Treasure Inside:" **my "God-wannabe" (see Chapter 8** for more details on the "God-wannabe").

Whereas my "Treasure Inside," a godly presence, wants to worship and commune with God **(See Chapter 9)**; my "God-wannabe," an evil presence, hates God and wants to take His place.

My "God-wannabe" has declared war on God, and wants to have dominion over me. He is made in the image of Satan, and entered into mankind in the Garden of Eden.

Both my "Treasure Inside" and my "God-wannabe" are unchangeable in nature. They will both exist in me exactly as they are until the day I go to be with the Lord.

On the other hand, my "Honeycomb" is the battleground between the two. It contains both "good roots" and "bad roots," and these roots can be transformed from "good" to "bad," and vice versa. **See Chapter 4.**

**The diagram below illustrates these multiple places.**

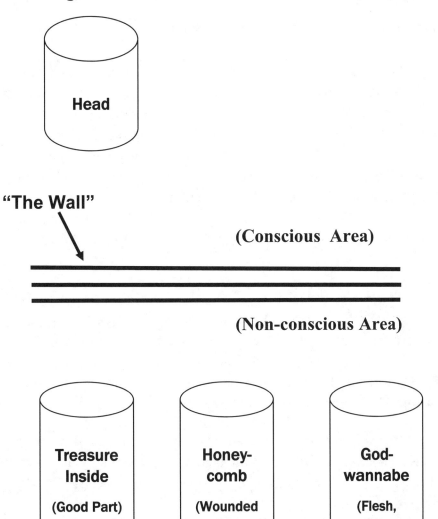

## How The War Progresses

Because it wants to become lord of my life, my "God-wannabe" attacks and plants a "bad root" in my "Honeycomb." That "bad root" then causes problems for me by producing "bad fruit."[67]

For Christians, what is supposed to happen is that my "Treasure Inside" sees the damage going on, and sends up a distress signal (the "oil light" comes on). Since my will power (a psychological attribute) has no authority to regulate or control what is going on inside my Nonconscious self, I need a solution that will occur below my level of consciousness to remove the "bad root." I can apply the blood of Jesus to the "bad root" (forgive and be forgiven) and thus have Jesus replace the "bad root" with His presence. He is well capable of doing this; but I need to take conscious action to bring that about. I need to "put oil in the engine."

This is the crucial battle, and it is where my will power has a irreplaceable role in my sanctification. I need to decide to forgive and be forgiven by Jesus. When I do this, Jesus has my permission to do His work. He will only come in if I invite Him, but He promises to do so if I ask Him. Then the transformation that occurs is a miracle performed by Him. There is no other way to be set free.

It is very important to recognize that I could not change myself by the exercise of my will. I am impotent to do this. But by the exercise of my will I bring Jesus in to change me.

Another metaphor might help make this clear. In my physical body, there is also a constant battle going on. There are entities that are intent on destroying my health (viruses, germs, toxins, etc.). Because of the presence of these destructive forces, the Lord gave me an immune

---

[67] The presence of our "God-wannabe" in us does not imply that we are "demon-possessed." Demons are separate entities from us. They are fallen angels, whereas our "God-wannabe" is part of us; because we are members of Adam's race.

system whose job it is to identify and destroy these attackers. In some situations my immune system needs a helping hand. Suppose I have an infection. I can consciously recognize that through the physical symptoms, and then decide to take an antibiotic to overcome the infection. However, I cannot by conscious force of will make the infection go away.

Likewise, if I discover that I have a "bad root" inside, I can consciously decide to apply the blood of Jesus to it. [68] But I cannot by conscious force of my will make the "bad root" go away.

In both the case of the war going on in my physical body and that going on in my Non-conscious self, I do need to become consciously aware that there is a problem so that I can decide to apply the appropriate "cure."

To succeed at this I need to do all of the following:

1. I need to sense, and to pay attention to, the signal sent up from my body or my "Treasure Inside."
2. I need to understand what that signal is telling me.
3. I need to trust that it is telling me the truth.
4. I need to apply the appropriate "cure:" (the anti-biotic in the case of an infection, or the blood of Jesus to the "bad root").

## Not Knowing About <u>Two</u> Presences

As the diagram illustrates, there are <u>two</u> presences below our level of consciousness. As a child, we didn't know that. So when we misbehaved, for instance by hitting another child, we were properly disciplined for doing that "bad" thing. We concluded that "I" did a bad thing. We blamed ourselves, and usually decided that everything below our level of conscious control was fickle and unreliable and "bad." Our

---

[68] Again, when I speak of **applying the blood of Jesus**, I am referring to the process of forgiving, being forgiven, having Jesus cleanse that place in my "Honeycomb," and fill that place with His presence.

"Treasure Inside" was condemned along with our "God-wannabe." We "threw the baby out with the bathwater." Our culture, and possibly our church, reinforced that perspective. So we tried as best we could to ignore or to control every message coming up from our Non-conscious Self.

## How To Lose The War

The way to lose the war is to ignore the "oil light" when it comes on. If I ignore the signal coming up from my "Treasure Inside," or don't understand what it is telling me, and/or don't trust that it is telling me the truth, I won't be able to apply the "cure." If I don't apply the "cure," the damage will remain there. If it is allowed to remain, the 'bad root' will begin to grow. Like a tumor, it will keep spreading unless it is destroyed.

> **Not paying attention to the signals from your "Treasure inside" and the Holy Spirit allows bad things to happen.**

Be assured that the objective of my "God-wannabe" is to win the war. He will always continue to attack and plant many more "bad roots." If I still don't take corrective action, he continues to gain more and more influence in my Honeycomb. More and more "bad fruit" will begin to manifest.

Eventually the damage grows to the point where it produces serious, observable problems in my life – for instance I might develop uncontrollable anger, or depression, or alcoholism, or a host of other problems.

## Which Is More Important?

Which is more important: your Conscious Self or your Non-conscious Self? That is like asking which is more important: your heart or your liver? The answer is that you have both because you need both. Your heart cannot do what your liver does, and your liver cannot do what your heart does.

Similarly, your Conscious attributes have a job to do, and so do your Non-conscious attributes. Your Conscious attributes cannot do what your Non-conscious attributes do, and vice versa.

In our culture, it is easy for us to see what your Head is good at: rational thinking and decision making. I won't elaborate on this, because you are well versed in this.

What is not so evident is the importance and purpose for your Non-conscious self. Science even recognizes the importance of your Non-conscious Self:

> "Huge amounts of evidence support the view that the 'conscious self' is in fact a very small portion of the mind's activity. Perception, abstract cognition, emotional processes, memory, and social interaction all appear to proceed to a great extent without the involvement of consciousness. Most of the mind is nonconscious. . . To put it another way, we are much, much more than our conscious processes." [69]

Part of that "much more" in this quote is the presence of God in your Non-conscious Self. As I have shown in the prior diagram, the presence of God is prominent in your Non-conscious Self. He has created your "Treasure Inside" in His image. When you became a Christian, He sent His Holy Spirit to dwell below your level of consciousness; and God is actively communicating with you through these faculties.

**In your Non-conscious self, you have access to the wisdom and presence of God!**

---

[69] Siegel, page 263.

**In other words, <u>below your level of consciousness you have at your disposal the wisdom and presence of God</u>.**

## Just think of that!

You need to respect both your Conscious Self and your Non-conscious self. You need all of those attributes to live your life, and that is why God gave them all to you. If you try to use the wrong attribute in a given situation, life will not go well.

# Both Presences Below Our Level Of Consciousness Seek To Influence Us [70]

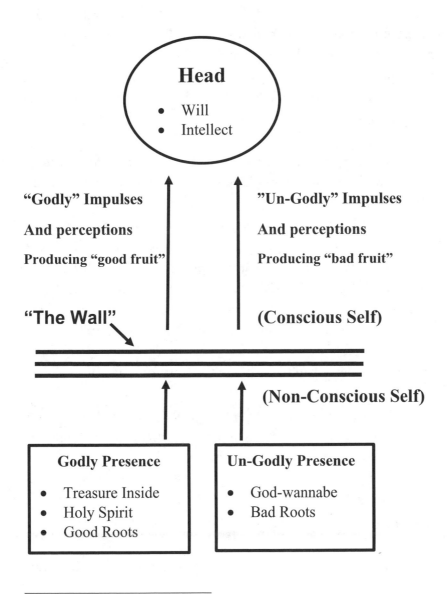

---

[70] The purpose of this diagram is simply to illustrate that there is within each of us both godly and ungodly entities, and they are each seeking to influence us. The diagram is not intended to try to be an exhaustive dissection of the great complexity inside us. Truly, we are fearfully and wonderfully made.

Note that I have labeled the influence of these presences as being "impulses and perceptions." I have done this because when the "Godly Presence" (the "mind of the Spirit") is in ascendance, we see things through those eyes and are impelled to act in life giving, Godly ways ("good fruit," Galatians 5:22-23). On the other hand, when the "Non-Godly Presence" (the "mind of the flesh") is in ascendance, we see things through those eyes and are impelled to act in ways that are sinful ("bad fruit," Galatians 5:19-21):

> *Now the works of the flesh are evident, which are: adultery, fornication, uncleanness, lewdness, idolatry, sorcery, hatred, contentions, jealousies, outbursts of wrath, selfish ambitions, dissensions, heresies, envy murders, drunkenness, revelries, and the like; of which I tell you beforehand, just as I also told you in time past, that those who practice such things will not inherit the kingdom of God. But the fruit of the Spirit is love, joy, peace, longsuffering, kindness, goodness, faithfulness, gentleness, self-control. Against such there is no law* (Galatians 5:19-23).

The Apostle Paul described the war and the fruit from it:

> *For the flesh lusts against the Spirit, and the Spirit against the flesh; and these are contrary to one another, so that you do not do the things that you wish* (Galatians 5:17).

## A Couple of Myths
In our culture, there are a couple of myths that I want to expose.

1. We tend to view our Conscious Selves as completely rational and reliable.
2. We see our Non-conscious Selves as fickle and unreliable.

# First myth:

Whether we know it or not, or like it or not, our conscious perception of reality is powerfully influenced by what goes on below our level of consciousness.

For example, suppose you tell a friend about a very personal problem you are having, and the friend reveals this confidential information to others. Would you be angry? Would this affect how you feel about that friend? Would you like to "give them a piece of your mind?"

With your logical mind (Head) you may argue that it is wisdom to re-evaluate your relationship. That would also be true; but is that what has influenced how you feel about them? Can you see how your rational perception has been influenced?

Or suppose that someone you know is on a football team. During the game, how do you feel about the players on the other team? Are you rational or non-emotional about them? Of course not. You are likely feeling very aggressive towards them, whereas you would not feel that same way if you just met one of them in a store.

It is impossible for us to be consciously neutral (completely rational) in emotionally powerful situations. The conditions in our "Honeycomb," that cause us to feel our emotions, powerfully influence our conscious mind. Science has proven this:

> "Emotion directly influences the functions of the entire brain and body, from physiological regulation to abstract reasoning" (Siegel, page 132).

Therefore, when our emotions come up (and despite how hard we may try not to feel them), both our "thinking" and our behavior are influenced. "Bad roots" that cause strong emotions give us strong impulses to "bad fruit." Sometimes the impulses are too strong to resist.

## Second Myth:

We also tend to view our Non-conscious Selves as unreliable. We don't trust what we sense. One of the reasons is that we lump all of our Non-conscious attributes together. We realize that we are sometimes impelled to do good things, and sometimes we are impelled to do bad things. We tend to think that all those contradictory impulses come from the same source – "me." We don't realize that there are <u>two</u> presences inside, and therefore two voices.

A second reason that we don't trust the signals coming up from inside is that we don't understand the language of our emotions. We were never taught this by anybody. It would be like me trying to fly an airplane on instruments. I have no training, and would undoubtedly crash and burn.

A third problem is that we haven't known what to do about the signals when we do hear them; because we haven't known how to apply the blood of Jesus to the "bad roots." Without knowing how to cure the problem when we hear about it, listening to the unpleasant feelings is painful; and we don't want to continue to hear them.

The bottom line is that the messages we receive from inside our Non-conscious Self are not unreliable or fickle. They accurately tell us what is going on <u>inside</u> there. Unfortunately, there is a war going on, and the messages give us strategic information about how the battle is going.

## A Big Mistake

Hopefully you can now see that if we distrust every message that comes up from our Non-conscious self, and thus try to use our "head" to rule our life, we get into trouble. Our "bad roots" grow and dominate more and more of our life.

Therefore, if somehow we can be convinced to ignore the signals coming up from our "Treasure Inside," our "God-wannabe" will have free reign, and we will be losing the war.

> **If we can be convinced to ignore the "signals" from our Treasure Inside, we will be losing the war!**

## No Teaching

Teaching on sanctification is rare in Christian preaching. How many times have you heard a sermon on the vital importance of sanctification, or how to appropriate it? How many books have you read that emphasize this, or TV programs that bring out the prominence of this phenomenal, miraculous, provision that Jesus gave to us? I have heard hundreds of teachings in various churches, and not once was this the focus. In fact, I went to a major seminary in the mid 90's, and the gift of sanctification was not mentioned even once.

> *So then faith comes by hearing, and hearing by the word of God*
> (Romans 10:17).

Somebody has to tell us about it if we are to know about it. And almost nobody is teaching about its importance, or how to appropriate it in our lives.

## Apply It!

Even if a person somehow learns of the importance of sanctification, they need to be taught how to apply it. Then they need to DO IT. Knowing about it is worthless unless one acts upon the knowledge.

Suppose you have a case of athlete's foot, and you buy a tube of anti-fungal cream. Then you go home and put the tube in a drawer. Periodically, when your feet are itching, you open the drawer, read the directions on the tube, and then put the tube back in the drawer. Then you complain that the cream doesn't work.

Now I realize that this is a silly scenario. How could you possibly believe that the cream will work unless you apply it? But that is exactly what it is like to study the Bible, and receive teaching about sanctification and how to apply it, and then NOT DO IT. You will not be sanctified.

## It Can Be Painful

Recognizing your bitter roots, honestly admitting the basis of sin behind them, repenting, forgiving, and being forgiven can be a painful

**The blood of Jesus will not sanctify you unless you apply it!**

process. But there is no shortcut to being set free.

I am a prayer counselor, and leading people through this process is what I do with them. However, people don't come for counseling unless they are in pain and life is not going well. They are motivated. The pain of the process of sanctification is less than the pain of their life. The writer of Hebrews said this so clearly:

> *If you endure chastening, God deals with you as with sons, for what son is there who a father does not chasten? But if you are without chastening, of which all have become partakers, then you are illegitimate and not sons. Furthermore, we have had human fathers who corrected us, and we paid them respect. Shall we not much more readily be in subjection to the Father of spirits and live? For they indeed for a few days chastened us as seemed best to them, but He for our profit, that we may be partakers of His holiness. Now no chastening seems to be joyful for the present, but painful; nevertheless,* afterward it yields the peaceable fruit of righteousness to those who have been trained by it (Hebrews 12:7-11).

Then he adds on:

> *Looking carefully lest anyone fall short of the grace of God; lest any root of bitterness springing up cause trouble, and by this many become defiled* (verse 15).

The author's implication is that it is a very good thing to suffer pain for your sin, because that will motivate you to seek His holiness. And His holiness is what He wants for you, and is why He died for you. The process is always painful, but it is the only path to holiness (sanctification). And when we have done this, we will feel peace and freedom and will be refreshed. It is rewarding.

A tragedy is that although we are all sinful and in need of sanctification, many are not in enough pain to pursue the transformation. Thus these are destined to be stuck in the same old ruts all their lives, displaying the same old bad fruit; because the blood of Jesus is the only way out.

In order to win the war that is going on, we need the provision to wash away our frequent sins that is only available in Jesus!

## Relationship With The Lord Enhanced

Our "Treasure Inside" is the part of us that is spirit, and thus communes with God. In the diagram on page 113, you can see this. As we win the war and improve our relationship with our "Treasure Inside," we will find ourselves having a more intimate relationship with God. This is a big deal, and a wonderful result of winning the war. This is how God intended for us to live.

# Chapter 11

## Christ-likeness Only Comes From God

## *You Can't Create It*

Recently I made a profound discovery. In several scriptures the writer speaks of the "faith of Christ," not "faith in Christ." At first glance this may seem unimportant. But the difference is very important. "Faith of Christ" clearly means that the faith has Christ as its source. In Greek when a noun is in the "genitive case," it indicates possession or source. In many scriptures "faith" and "Christ" are in the genitive case." Here the message is that our faith has Christ as its source. [71] It is Christ's faith, not ours, that He imparts to us.

I had always thought the Bible was saying it was up to me to sort of crank up my faith in Christ. "Faith in Christ" can be interpreted that way. But as I review my own life experience, for example I clearly see that when I made Jesus my Lord, there was something that rose up from inside me that convinced me He is who He said He is. I didn't put that faith there. God did.

This awareness makes it clear that I am much more dependent on Christ than I had thought. This opens up a whole new issue. If I want my faith to increase, which of course I do, how does that happen? Am I just passive in this, waiting for God to impart it, or is there a way for me to participate in developing more faith?

---

[71] "Faith in Christ" would need to be in the dative case. Unfortunately, most modern English translations translate the genitive case as "in" rather than "of." This is inaccurate and misleading. The scriptures with genitive case ("of"): Rom. 3:22, Gal 2:16 twice, Galatians 3:22, Eph 3:12, Phil 3:9, Jas 2:1, Rev 14:12. Scriptures with dative case ("in"): Act 24:24, Gal 3:26, Eph 1:15,Col 1:4, Col 2:5, 2 Tim 3:15.

A key scripture in this is Galatians 5:22-23:

*And the fruit of the Spirit is love, joy, peace, longsuffering, kindness, goodness, faith, meekness, temperance: gentleness, self-control. Against such there is no law* (Young's Literal Translation).

## Some key points about this scripture:

These desirable attributes are the fruit of the Spirit. The words "fruit of the Spirit" is genitive singular. The genitive case indicates possession or source, so this "good fruit" has its origin in the Spirit as its source. Singular says all those things listed are various words describing the fruit (singular) of the Spirit. They are the way that the presence of the Spirit manifests itself. The degree to which these attributes are consistently manifest in your life is the degree to which you have been transformed into the image of Jesus; because Jesus and the Spirit have identical Godly attributes, and these are some of them. Jesus indeed had faith. So the more Christ-like you have become, the more these attributes will be consistently manifest in your life. [72]

Conversely, to the degree that these attributes are not consistently manifest in your life, to that degree you have still the need to be transformed. It is important to recognize that we are all in process. [73]

---

[72] Some additional New Testament scriptures that list Godly traits are: Ephesians 5:9; Colossians 3:12; 1 Timothy 6:11; 2 Peter 1:5-7.

[73] The Greek word translated here as "faith" is *pistis* (Strong's # 4102) which is a noun. Some translations have "faithfulness" here, but that is inaccurate. "Faithfulness" would be Greek *pistos* (Strong's #4103) which is an adjective. I think this difference matters, because "faith" is a concrete attribute of God, whereas "faithfulness" is merely a description of a noun. Most importantly, the Greek has the noun *pistis*, and we should stick to the actual grammar whenever possible.

Note that "faith" is one of these good attributes. The implication is clear that as we become more and more like Jesus, we will display more and more of these attributes. This means that the more we work out our

> **The way to increase your faith is to continue to be sanctified!**

sanctification, our "faith" (among others of these attributes) will increase. So we can participate in increasing our own "faith" by having a lifestyle of applying the blood of Jesus to our sins! And in this process it is actually God that is changing you.

> *Therefore, my beloved, as you have always obeyed, not as in my presence only, but now much more in my absence, work out your own salvation with fear and trembling; for it is God who works in you both to will and to do for His good pleasure* (Philippians 2:12-13).

Here Paul is not advocating that the readers obey by producing "good fruit" with their will power. He is encouraging them to obey his teaching, which means to "work out their own salvation," which is their sanctification.

## Faking it

With our will power, we can occasionally imitate these attributes, but not consistently. In our own strength we cannot replace the spiritual transformation that is only available through the sacrifice of Jesus. As described in **Chapter 3**, the spiritual reality is overwhelmingly overpowering to our willpower. "Good fruit" can only come from a "good root," which is Jesus inside us.

The message in this is that if we do not consistently produce one or more aspects of the fruit of the Spirit (or if it is a lot of work to do so), the "good root" isn't there. **See Chapter 4**. Then you need to be absolutely honest with yourself and the Lord, and ask Him to show you what the "bad root" is that is causing the "bad fruit" in your life. He loves you and wants to help you get set free from the sin. The absence of Christ-like qualities

> **Don't "fake it."**
> **Let Jesus**
> **transform you.**

should not impel you to try hard to be good using your will power (which it usually does). It should impel you to focus on your process of sanctification.

There is no other answer. As you are sanctified, the new attributes effortlessly all emanate from Christ inside you. Can you see how pervasive is the evil nature within us, and how fundamentally important it is to embrace the process of sanctification that Christ sacrificed Himself to provide for you?

# Chapter 12

# A Pattern for Prayer

## *Following The Lord's Leading*

## Pay Attention To <u>Every</u> Negative Emotion

The Lord will lead you in how to pray by sending up emotions that tell you what is going on inside. If you will begin to pay attention to what He is telling you through your emotions, you will be walking the path of transformation into the image of Jesus. To start with, it may seem laborious and may take some time. But as you practice this, you will find yourself more easily understanding the process. Most importantly, realize that the emotions are not random, unimportant events. They are in fact the way the Lord will lead you in your transformation.

To begin with, the Lord will likely only have you deal with current issues. For instance, a driver may pull out in front of you and endanger you. You feel angry. You have judged that other driver and need to forgive them. The problem and solution are easy to see.

At some point He will begin to take you deeper, to old wounds buried inside, and that is more complex. [74] But He won't take you there until you are ready. So rest in the assurance that He is in charge of your process. You are not in this alone.

> **As the Lord takes you deeper, you may want to read my book "I Will Give You Rest" to help you go to the deeper places.**

---

[74] This book is intended to get you started on your sanctification process. It is a primer of sorts. Once the Lord starts to take you to deeper issues, you need my book "I Will Give You Rest" which will guide you on the deeper journey.

To begin with, you may only be aware of your negative emotions when they are really big. Go with that. However, be aware that subtle negative emotions also give you important information; and as you practice this process, you will become more aware of more mild emotions. In fact, the majority of negative emotions that you feel will be fairly mild. Do not skip them because they are mild. They are still indicating a need to apply the blood of Jesus.

For instance, you may be a bit irritated because your wife left the top off the toothpaste tube, but you may not be so angry as to start an argument. Nevertheless, this emotion is still a signal that you judged her, and so you need to pray. Otherwise these little bitter roots will accumulate (a bundle of bitter roots will be forming inside you), and at some point you may explode at her over something minor.

Because we are human, these sorts of mild reactions happen many times a day, and we therefore need to pray many times a day. If we do this we don't have to carry the burden of those sinful reactions, because Jesus takes them. We then experience the rest that Jesus promised.

---

**A Profound Way For God To Lead You:**

**If you will diligently listen and pray as outlined below, this will provide a simple, accurate, and effectual way for God to direct your walk of sanctification. He knows what He wants you to deal with, and will lead you by your emotions.**

# How To Listen To Your Emotions And Pray

<u>**Pay Attention**</u> to every **negative emotion** you feel.

<u>**Keep a pad of paper with you**</u> to write down <u>every</u> incident of a negative emotion, no matter how small.  It can be a short note or a long journal.  It is your choice.

A major purpose of keeping a written list is so that if at the end of the day your paper is blank, you will know **you haven't been listening**.  We all judge (and therefore have a negative emotion) many times every day.  It is very easy to fall back into the old pattern of not listening if we aren't watchful.

<u>**Pray over each item on your list**</u>.  Be diligent to set aside time to get quiet and comfortable where there are a minimum of distractions.

- Look at each item on the list.  Close your eyes and remember the recent incident that triggered the negative emotion.
- Let the emotion come up, and choose a "feeling" word to describe the emotion. Most negative emotions are signals that you have judged.  If you need help naming the emotion, see the list of emotions below.  This may be difficult for you at first.  Saying something like: "I feel like she didn't listen" is not a feeling.  It is a conclusion.
- For deep, strong emotions, spend some time (maybe 15 minutes total) writing about what you are feeling.  What you choose to write about should be extremely personal and important to you. Write continuously: Do not worry about punctuation, spelling, and grammar. If you run out of things to say draw a line or repeat what you have already written. Keep pen on paper.  Write only for yourself: You may plan to destroy or hide what you are

writing. This exercise is for your eyes only. The act of writing seems to strengthen your deep connection with the event and your reaction. You are listening to yourself and expressing what is deep inside.

- Forgive whomever/whatever you have judged.
- If your Treasure Inside is the one you have judged, ask him/her to forgive you (If you have a history of judging yourself, once you begin to listen you may be astonished at how awful you are to yourself.)
- Ask the Lord to forgive you for the judgment, and
  - To remove the bitter root
  - To cleanse that place with His blood
  - To fill that place with His spirit.

**After you pray**, review the incident in your mind and see if there is peace. If there is peace, you are done. If not, there is more praying to be done. The further praying may have to do with the current event, or there may be an older, deeper root to be prayed about. When you have peace, you are done. Peace means that the work the Lord wanted you to do right now is done. It does not necessarily mean that every bitter root with respect to that person or type of situation is gone. If there is more, in due season the Lord will bring it up. He is actively leading you.

> **As you can see, this is a completely new lifestyle, in comparison to your old way – for the rest of your life!**

Once you have prayed <u>and have peace</u>, then just go on and <u>enjoy the day</u>. At that point you have done all that the Lord is wanting you to do for the moment. Do not go digging around looking for dirt. He will give you another negative emotion when it is time to do more.

> **Once you have prayed <u>and have peace</u>, then just go on and <u>enjoy the day</u>. At that point you have done all that the Lord is wanting you to do for the moment.**
>
> **He wants the healing process to be a joy, not a burden.**

In praying this way you are recognizing that what was going wrong was a spiritual issue, and you have applied the spiritual cure that Jesus has provided:

> *Finally, my brethren, be strong in the Lord and in the power of His might. Put on the whole armor of God, that you may be able to stand against the wiles of the devil. For we do not wrestle against flesh and blood, but against principalities, against powers, against the rulers of the darkness of this age, against spiritual hosts of wickedness in heavenly places. Therefore take up the whole armor of God, that you may be able to withstand in the evil day, and having done all, to stand* (Ephesians 6:10-13).

### <u>Positive Emotions</u>

Also listen to your <u>positive emotions</u>, because they are also directional. They point you towards things that are good for you.

It is not selfish to listen to your positive emotions. Of course, no healing prayer is necessary, because they are not pointing out sin. <u>Just enjoy them!</u> They mean that good things are happening; and this can be an opportunity for thanksgiving and praise to the Lord.

## WARNING

It is especially important that you approach this exercise with the correct perspective.

It is not something you are initiating and accomplishing. Therefore it is not a legalistic routine.

Rather, the negative emotions are a tool that the Lord uses to guide us. He puts you in situations which will trigger a certain negative emotion. He is the One speaking to you through your emotion.

You are simply responding to His prompting. That is why it is so important to be listening.

Your emotions are a robust way for God to guide you personally, in the moment. The emotions are not random. He uses them to bring about transformation in your life.

As you begin to listen to Him, and respond, your relationship with Him will be enhanced.

If there are no negative emotions, He isn't speaking to you right then. Then just relax and enjoy life. He will be faithful to let you know the next time He has healing work for you to do.

## List Of Negative and Positive Emotions

Note that Anger is always an umbrella covering another feeling. When you feel anger, you need to look underneath it to find the underlying feeling. In the list below, the feelings listed under "Anger" are the most common feelings that are underlying it. At the same time, be aware that many of the "Other Negative" emotions can also manifest themselves as anger. For healing to come one must feel what is behind the anger, so that you know the nature of the sin.

| **Anger** | **Other** | | |
|---|---|---|---|
| Belittled | **Negative** | Defeated | Fussy |
| Betrayed | Abhorrence | Defensive | Gloomy |
| Controlled | Agitated | Defiled | Gossipy |
| Cross | Aggravated; | Demeaned | Grasping |
| Disvalued | Alarmed | Depressed | Greedy |
| Exasperated | Aloof | Desolate | Grieved |
| Fear | Annoyed | Desperate | Grim |
| Fearful | Anxious | Despondent | Half-hearted |
| Frustrated | Apathetic | Different | Hate |
| Furious | Apprehensive | Dirty | Helpless |
| Grouchy | Ashamed | Disappointed | Hesitant |
| Ignored | Attacked | Discontented | Homesick |
| Indignant | Aversion | Disgusted | Hopeless |
| Insecure | Baffled | Dislike | Hurt |
| Mad | Belittled | Disdain | Impatient |
| Not heard | Bewildered | Domineering | Inadequate |
| Powerless | Bitter | Doomed | Incapable |
| Threatened | Blah | Dull | Incompetent |
| Unimportant | Boastful | Edgy | Indifferent |
| | Bored | Egotistical | Inferior |
| | Callous | Embarrassed | Inflexible |
| | Cautious | Envious | Inhibited |
| | Confused | Exhausted | Insecure |
| | Conniving | Fiendish | Insignificant |
| | Contempt | Foolish | Intimidated |
| | Cranky | Forlorn | Intolerant |
| | Creepy | Forgetful | Irritable |
| | | Friendless | Isolated |

Jealous
Lazy
Lethargic
Listless
Lonely
Lustful
Mangy
Martyred
Mean
Mediocre
Melancholy
Merciless
Meticulous
Miserly
Misjudged
Misunderstood
Morose
Mournful
Muddled
Mystified
Naked

Nauseated
Neglected
Nervous
Obstinate
Out of control
Out of place
Overcome
Overworked
Panicky
Paralyzed
Passive
Perplexed
Pooped
Pressured
Reluctant
Repulsed
Resentful
Resigned
Restless
Restrained
Ridiculous

Sad
Sarcastic
Scheming
Seductive
Self-conscious
Shabby
Shaky
Shy
Sick
Skeptical
Small
Stubborn
Sulky
Suspicious
Tearful
Tempted
Tense
Terrified
Threatened
Timid
Tired

Traumatized
Troubled
Two-faced
Undone
Uncaring
Uncertain
Unconcerned
Uneasy
Un-loveable
Upset
Unglued
Unstable
Unsure
Unwanted
Uptight
Vulnerable
Weary
Wilted
Worried
Worthless

## **Positive Emotions**

Admired
Affirmed
Alive
Ambitious
Amused
Appreciated
Approved
Astonished
Awed
Belonging
Blessed
Bold
Brave

Calm
Carefree
Cheerful
Comfortable
Compassion-
      ate
Confident
Considerate
Contented
Cooperative
Courageous
Creative
Curious

Delighted
Desire
Determined
Eager
Ecstasy
Efficient
Elated
Empowered
Encouraged
Energetic
Enjoyment
Enthusiastic
Euphoric

Excited
Expectant
Exuberant
Free
Friendly
Generous
Gentle
Glad
Gracious
Grateful
Happy
Helpful
Hopeful

Hospitable
Important
Impressed
Independent
Inspired
Interested
Irresistible
Joyful
Kind
Liked
Longing
Love
Loveable
Mellow
Merciful
Merry
Met
Open
Optimistic
Overjoyed
Patient
Peaceful
Pleasure
Reasonable
Relaxed
Romantic
Safe
Satisfaction
Secure
Self-assured
Sensible
Sensitive
Sensual
Sentimental
Serene
Serious
Soft
Sophisticated

Sure
Sympathetic
Talkative
Tender
Tenacious
Thankful
Thrilled
Tranquil
Transparent
Triumphant
Unbiased
Under-
standing
Understood
Validated
Valued
Vibrant
Yearning

# What Next?
## *There Is More!*

Hopefully, now that you understand the "mystery of the ages" that Jesus revealed, you can have victory over sin through His great gifts to humanity.

My suggestions about what is next are therefore:

1. First, keep praying as outlined in Chapter 12, for the rest of your life. Jesus died so that you could have ongoing victory over sin.

2. Second, if after reading this book you have experienced the transforming power of Jesus, you might want to dig deeper and allow Him to set you free of any of your life patterns that are not what you are pleased with. Most of us have some such issues going on.

    **If so, you will benefit from my first book, "I Will Give You Rest" and the Workbook that goes along with it.** It is parallel with this book, and covers some of the same basic principles, but then it goes deeper to show you how to get free of any besetting problems. You can get a copy on Amazon.com, or by going to my website: www.divinelydesigned.com.

> **To go deeper, get my other book, "I Will Give You Rest"- there is more to learn.**

    I pray that you will continue on the journey of transformation that Jesus made possible, and that you will find it to be an exciting and rewarding and victorious journey.

# Appendix A

## *A Potential Obstacle*

There is a theological teaching that says that when we become a Christian, all of our sins are forgiven. This implies that when we receive the first gift (become a child of God), the second gift occurs simultaneously (at that moment we are forgiven for all past, present, and future sins). **This is a huge error**. If this is something you have been taught, that would make it difficult for you to accept the fact that forgiveness of our sins is a lifelong process – the second aspect of our gift from Jesus.

This perspective is in error for several reasons:

- First, the New Testament does not contain support for this position. [75]

- Second, if that perspective was the case, one would have to ignore huge scriptural evidence to the contrary, including the 184 places in the Epistles (Romans through Jude), written to Christians, which specifically state that our being set free from sin is a lifelong process. [76]

- Third, if all our sins were forgiven, one would have to ignore the fact that many Christians struggle with the consequences of long past sins until they repent, forgive, and are forgiven.

---

[75] One scripture often presented as proof that all of our sins are forgiven is Colossians 2:13: *And you, being dead in your trespasses and the uncircumcision of your flesh, He has made alive together with Him, having forgiven you all trespasses.* This is a mistranslation. The Greek has "forgiving" as a participle. A correct rendering would be: *forgiving you all trespasses.* The implication therefore is a continuing process.

[76] For example: *If we say that we have no sin, we deceive ourselves, and the truth is not in us. If we confess our sins, He is faithful and just to forgive us our sins and to cleanse us from all unrighteousness* (1 John 1:8-9).

- Fourth, this perspective would imply that I do not need to repent of sins I commit in the future, since they have already been forgiven. This would then mean we would have to ignore all the scriptures that tell us that we need to forgive in order to be forgiven. After all, if all my sins are already forgiven, I wouldn't have to do anything to be cleansed of my sins. Taking this logic even further, it implies that since my sins are already forgiven, I am free to continue sinning and will have no negative consequences. Of course, this is an outrageous idea, and it contradicts the many scriptures about the deadly consequences of sin. [77]

If you are not yet convinced of the need for ongoing sanctification, in **Appendix B** I have included most of the passages that refer to the sanctification process. To deny that Christians need ongoing sanctification <u>would require ignoring all these passages.</u>

If you are still not yet sure what is the truth about this issue, the best way to learn the truth is to read the Epistles of the New Testament (Romans through Jude) for yourself, rather than reading what someone else says about this. **As you read, keep in mind that the Epistles were written to people who were already Christians, just like you.** You will discover that Jesus has in fact made it possible for our sins to be forgiven (and mankind never before had that available), but it will also be clear that forgiveness for sins is an ongoing process for the children of God. Reading the Epistles is how I myself found out about the truth.

Another way to get a greater understanding of this issue is to read my book, "Exceedingly Great and Precious Promises." There I

---

[77] All sin is deadly. For example: *What then? Shall we sin because we are not under law but under grace? Certainly not! Do you not know that to whom you present yourselves slaves to obey, you are that one's slaves whom you obey, whether of sin leading to death, or of obedience leading to righteousness* (Romans 6:15-16). And: *For the wages of sin is death, but the gift of God is eternal life in Christ Jesus our Lord* (Romans 6:23).

delve further into this issue. I also explain the reasons why the process of sanctification has been widely ignored in the Western Christian church. I think the reasons will surprise you.

# Appendix B

## *Scriptural Evidence*

Scripture is the proof of the importance of transformation into the image of Jesus, and that evidence is what I intend to present here.

There are two aspects of what is referred to as "salvation."

1. First, there is the **one-time event** that occurred when I gave my life to Jesus and became a child of God. This also secures my place in heaven after I die.
2. Second, there is the **ongoing process** whereby in this life I can be gradually changed into the image of Jesus through His ongoing sacrifice for my sins.

As I began to study the New Testament (second chapter of Acts through Jude, which covers the time of the church age) to see what emphasis the writers placed on each of these aspects of "salvation," I had a reason to believe that the emphasis would be on the one-time event. After all, that is currently the major

> **The ongoing process is overwhelmingly emphasized in the Epistles!**

emphasis in the Christian church, to the virtual exclusion of the ongoing process.

I was astounded, as I discovered **exactly the reverse**: the ongoing process is overwhelmingly emphasized! In my study, the ongoing process is spoken of many more times than is the one-time event (the ratio is the number of salvation occurrences that refer to the process of sanctification divided by the number that refer to the one-time event). The ratio depends on how you count.

## Summary of frequency of occurrences:

|  | Ongoing | One-time | Ratio |
|---|---|---|---|
| Based on the Greek words: | 134 | 24 | 5 times |
| Based on # passages | 151 | 16 | 9 times |
| Based on # verses | 184 | 19 | 10 times |

The "passages" are listed below. Quite a number of those "passages" contain more than one "verse," so there are more "verses" than "passages" in the above comparison.

One way to put this ratio in perspective is to realize that in my New King James Version of the Bible, from the second chapter of Acts through Jude, there are only 153 pages. This means there are as many passages about transformation into the image of Jesus as there are pages in these Epistles.

This result doesn't mean that the one-time event is unimportant. It simply means that the writers of the Epistles were obviously highly motivated to emphasize the ongoing process.

If this result is a surprise to you – and I think it should be – I encourage you to read the scriptures that I have listed below. This listing is where I arrived at the # passages and # verses in the above comparison. The translation I have used is the New King James Version. Underlining is mine, as is content in parentheses. In some places I have inserted my own translation.

Where ever I have inserted (continuously) it is because the Greek is in the "present tense," which refers to continuous or repeated action, as opposed to a one-time action. As you will see, there are many places where this distinction will add greatly to our understanding of a passage.

# Section 1

The passages in this Section clearly speak of the process whereby we are changed into the image of Jesus:

- *But now having been set free from sin, and having become slaves of God, you have your fruit to holiness, and the end, everlasting life. For the wages of sin is death, but the gift of God is eternal life in Christ Jesus our Lord* (Romans 6:22-23),

    "And now, having been freed from sin, and having become servants to God, you all are continuously possessing your fruit as a consequence of sanctification, and the goal abiding life. For what one earns from sin is death, but the gracious free gift of God is abiding life in Christ Jesus our Lord" (Romans 6:22-23, <u>My Translation</u>).

- *For whom He foreknew, He also predestined <u>to be conformed to the image of His Son</u>, that He might be the firstborn among many brethren* (Romans 8:29-30).

- *And as we have borne the image of the man of dust, <u>we shall also bear the image of the heavenly Man </u>*(1 Corinthians 15:49)<u>.</u>

- *Now the Lord is the Spirit; and where the Spirit of the Lord is, there is liberty. But we all, with unveiled face, beholding as in a mirror the glory of the Lord, are being* [continuously] <u>transformed into the same image</u> *from glory to glory, just as by the Spirit of the Lord* ( 2 Corinthians 3:17).

- *Therefore, if anyone is in Christ, <u>he is a new creation</u>; old things have passed away; behold all things have become new* (2 Corinthians 5:17).

- *My little children, for whom I labor in birth again until <u>Christ is formed in you </u>*(Galatians 4:19).

- *For in Christ Jesus neither circumcision nor uncircumcision avails anything, but <u>a new creation</u>* (Galatians 6:15)<u>.</u>

- *According as he hath chosen us in him before the foundation of the world, that we should be holy* [<u>us to continuously be holy</u>] *and without blame before him in love* (Ephesians 1:4 KJV).

- *For we* [continuously] *are His workmanship,* [being] *created in Christ Jesus for good works, which God prepared beforehand that we should walk in them* (Ephesians 2:10).

    "For we continuously are His workmanship, <u>being created</u> in Christ Jesus resulting in good works, which God prepared beforehand that we might be able to walk in them. [because He is in the process of changing us into His image, wherever this has occurred inside our Non-conscious Selves, this "good root" makes it possible for us to continuously produce "good fruit."]( Ephesians 2:10 <u>My Translation</u> and elaboration).

- *. . . till we all come to the unity of the faith and of the knowledge of the Son of God, to <u>a perfect man</u>, to the measure of <u>the stature of the fullness of Christ</u>* (Ephesians 4:13).

- *. . . and be renewed in the spirit of your mind, and that you put on <u>the new man which was created according to God, in true righteousness and holiness</u>* (Ephesians 4:23-24).

  ". . . yet continuously having yourself being renewed in the spirit of your conscious mind, and be <u>putting on the new man</u>, having been created down from God in righteousness and kindness of the truth "(Ephesians 4:23-24, <u>My Translation</u>).

- *. . . in the body of His flesh through death <u>to present you holy, and blameless</u>, and above reproach in His sight – if indeed you continue in the faith, grounded and steadfast, and are not* [continuously] *moved away from the hope of the gospel which you heard, which was preached to every creature under heaven, of which I, Paul, became a minister* (Colossians 1:22-23).

- *To them God willed to make known what are the riches of the glory of this mystery among the gentiles: <u>which</u>* [continuously] *<u>is Christ in you, the hope of glory</u>* (Colossians 1:27).

- *Him we* [are continuously preaching] *preach, warning every man and* [continuously teaching] *teaching every man in all wisdom, that we may present every man <u>perfect in Christ Jesus</u>* (Colossians 1:28).

- *. . . and have put on <u>the new man</u> who is renewed in knowledge <u>according to the image of Him</u> who created him* (Colossians 3:10). *And have clothed yourselves with <u>the new [spiritual self]</u>, which is (ever in the process of being) renewed and remolded into (fuller and more perfect knowledge upon) knowledge, <u>after the image (the likeness) of Him</u> Who created it* (Colossians 3:10, Amplified).

- *Epaphras, who is one of you, a bondservant of Christ, greets you, always laboring fervently for you in prayers, that you may stand <u>perfect and complete</u> in all the will of God* (Col. 4:12)

- *For this is the will of God, your sanctification; that you should abstain from sexual immorality* (1 Thessalonians 4:3).

- *Now may the God of peace Himself <u>sanctify you completely</u>; and may your whole spirit, soul, and body be preserved <u>blameless</u> at the coming of our Lord Jesus Christ.* (1 Thessalonians 5:23).

- *For both He who* [continuously] *sanctifies and those who are* <u>[continuously] *being sanctified*</u> *are all of one, for which reason He is not ashamed to call them brethren* (Hebrews 2:11).

- *For they indeed for a few days chastened us as seemed best to them, but He for our profit, that <u>we may be partakers of His holiness.</u> Now no chastening seems to be joyful for the present, but painful; nevertheless afterward it yields the peaceable fruit of righteousness to those who have been trained by it* (Hebrews 12:10-11).

   "And all chastening for the present, indeed, does not seem to be of joy, but of sorrow, yet through her (the chastening) she is continuously giving righteousness to the ones having been so exercised" (Hebrews 12:11, <u>My Translation</u>).

- *Follow peace with all men and holiness, without which no man shall see the Lord: Looking diligently lest any man fail of The grace of God; lest any root of bitterness springing up trouble you, and thereby many be defiled* (Hebrews 12:14-15, KJV).

   ". . . with all, [speaking of the process of transformation into holiness in verse 10] continuously pursue peace and sanctification, apart from which no one shall see the Lord." (Hebrews 12:14 <u>My translation</u>).

- *. . . by which have been given to us exceedingly great and precious promises, that through these <u>you may be partakers of the divine nature</u>, having escaped the corruption that is in the world through lust* (2 Peter 1:4).

- *Now to Him who is able to keep you from stumbling, and to <u>present you faultless</u> before the presence of His glory with exceeding joy, to God our savior, Who alone is wise, be glory and majesty, dominion and power, both now and forever. Amen* ( Jude 24).

# Section 2

The passages in this Section clearly refer to continuous transformation, not a one-time event. I have inserted [continuously] wherever the Greek verb indicates that. If the verb is "continuous," it obviously cannot be referring to the one-time event.

- *"And by Him everyone who* [continuously] *believes is* [continuously] *justified from all things from which you could not be justified by the law of Moses"* (Acts 13:39).
- *But now the righteousness of God apart from the law is revealed, being witnessed by the Law and the Prophets, even the righteousness of God, through faith in Jesus Christ, to all and on all who believe. For there is no difference: for all have sinned and fall short of the glory of God, <u>being</u> [continuously] <u>justified</u> freely by His grace through the redemption that is in Christ Jesus, whom God set forth as a propitiation by His blood, through faith, to demonstrate His righteousness, because in His forbearance God had passed over the sins that were previously committed, to demonstrate at the present time His righteousness, that He might be just and the <u>justifier</u> [<u>the one continuously justifying</u>] <u>of the one</u> who has faith in Jesus* (Romans 3:21-26).
- *Therefore we* [continuously] *conclude that a man is* [continuously] *justified by faith apart from the deeds of the law* (Romans 3:28).
- "We were buried together, then, with Him through the baptism into death, that even as Christ was raised up out of the dead through the glory of the Father, so also we, in newness of life, live our lives. For, if we have become united together [with Christ] in the likeness of His death, so also <u>we shall exist [in the likeness] of the resurrection.</u> Continuously knowing this, that our old man has been crucified with Him, that the body of sin may be made useless, so that sin is no longer continuously enslaving us. For he who has died has been set free from sin. And if we died with Christ, we are continuously believing that we also shall live together with Him" (Romans 6:4-8, <u>My Translation</u>).
- "So also you all, be continuously occupying yourselves to indeed being continuously dead to sin, and continuously living in God in Jesus Christ our Lord. 1n this manner, be not continuously letting sin reign in your mortal body, to be continuously obeying it in its powerful impulses; You all also do not be continuously manifesting your members as weapons of ungodliness in sin, but

on the contrary manifest yourselves in God, in that way continuously living separated out of the dead, and your members weapons of righteousness in God; for your sin shall not have lordship, for you all are not continuously under law, but under grace. What then? Shall we sin seeing that we are not continuously under law but continuously under grace? Let it not be! Have you all not known that to whom you all are continuously presenting yourselves as slaves into obedience, slaves you all are to him to whom you all are continuously obeying, whether of sin into death, or of obedience into righteousness? But thanks be to God, that you all were continuously slaves of sin, yet you all obeyed from the heart the type of teaching to which you all were given; and having been freed from sin, you all are enslaved to righteousness" (Romans 6:11-18, My Translation).

- *Do you not know that to whom you* [continuously] *present yourselves slaves to obey, you* [continuously] *are the one's slaves whom you* [continuously] *obey, whether of sin leading to death, or of obedience leading to righteousness?* (Romans 6:16).

- *Therefore, my brethren, you also have become dead to the law through the body of Christ, that you may be married to another – to Him who was raised from the dead, that we should bear fruit to God . . . But now we have been delivered from the law, having died to what we were held by, so that we should serve in the newness of the Spirit and not in the oldness of the letter* (Romans 7:4, 6).

   "In the same way, my brethren, you all also are made to die to the law through the body of the Christ, making you all to become different, being roused out of the dead, that we bear fruit with God. . . but now we have been freed from the law of death, (in which we had been continuously held down), so that now <u>we will continuously be servants in newness of spirit</u>, and not in the oldness of letter of the Law." (Romans 7:4, 6: My translation).

- *That the righteous requirement of the law might be fulfilled in us who do not* [continuously] *walk according to the flesh but according to the Spirit* (Romans 8:4).

- *But you are not in the flesh but in the Spirit, if indeed <u>the Spirit of God</u>* [continuously] *<u>dwells in you</u>. Now if anyone does not have the Spirit of Christ, he is not His* (Romans 8:9).

- *But if the Spirit of Him who raised Jesus from the dead* [continuously] *<u>dwells in you</u>, He who raised Christ from the dead will also give life to your mortal bodies through His Spirit who dwells in you* (Romans 8:11).

- *For we are saved by hope; but hope that is* [continuously] *seen* [continuously] *is not hope; for what a man* [continuously] *seeth, why doth he yet* [continuously] *hope for?* (Romans 8:24, KJV).

- *That if you confess with your mouth the Lord Jesus and believe in your heart that God has raised Him from the dead, you will be saved. For with the heart one* [continuously] *believes unto righteousness, and with the mouth confession is* [continuously] *made unto salvation. For the Scripture* [continuously] *says, "Whoever* [continuously] *believes on Him will not be put to shame"* (Romans 10:9-11).

- *And do not be* [continuously] *conformed to this world, but be* [continuously] *<u>transformed</u> by the renewing of your mind that you may* [continuously] *prove what is the good and acceptable and perfect will of God* (Romans 12:2. Underlining is mine)

- [Continuously] *Owe no one anything except to* [continuously] *love one another, for he who* [continuously] *loves another has fulfilled the law* (Romans 13:8).

- *For the message of the cross is foolishness to those who are perishing, but to us who are* [continuously] *being saved it is the power of God* (1 Corinthians 1:18).

- *It pleased God through the foolishness of the message preached to save those who* [continuously] *believe* (1 Corinthians 1:21)

- *By which also you are* [continuously] *saved, if you hold fast that word which I preached to you – unless you* [continuously] *believed in vain* (1 Corinthians 15:2).

- *For we are to God the fragrance of Christ among those who are* [continuously] *being saved and among those who are* [continuously] *perishing* (2 Corinthians 2:15).

- *Who also hath made us able ministers of the new testament; not of the letter, but of the spirit; for the letter* [continuously kills] *killeth, but the spirit* [is continuously making us alive] *giveth life* (2 Corinthians 3:6 KJV).

- *Therefore we do not lose heart. Even though our outward man is perishing, yet the inward man is being* [continuously] *renewed day by day* (2 Corinthians 4:16).

- *For He made Him who knew no sin to be sin for us, that we might* [continuously be becoming] *become the righteousness of God in Him* (2 Corinthians 5:21).

- *Therefore,* [continuously] *having these promises, beloved, let us cleanse ourselves from all filthiness of the flesh and spirit,* [continuously] *perfecting holiness in the fear of God* (2 Corinthians 7:1).

- *Finally, brethren, farewell.* [Continuously] *become complete.* [Continuously] *be of good comfort,* [continuously] *be of one mind,* [continuously] *live in peace; and the God of love and peace will be with you* (2 Corinthians 13:11).

- *"For I through the law died to the law that I might live to God. I have been crucified with Christ; it is no longer I who* [continuously] *live, but Christ* [continuously] *lives in me; and the life which I now* [continuously] *live in the flesh I* [continuously] *live by faith in the Son of God, who loved me and gave Himself for me. I do not* [continuously] *set aside the grace of God; for if righteousness comes through the law, then Christ died in vain."* (Galatians 2:19-21).

- *For the flesh* [continuously] *lusts against the Spirit, and the Spirit against the flesh; and these are* [continuously] *contrary to one another, so that you do not* [continuously] *do the things that you* [continuously] *wish. But if you are* [continuously being] *led by the Spirit, you are not* [continuously] *under the law* (Galatians 5:17-18).

- *In Him we* [continuously] *have redemption through His blood, the forgiveness of sins, according to the riches of His grace* (Ephesians 1:7).

- *Which* [continuously] *is His body, the fullness of Him who* [continuously] *fills all in all* (Ephesians 1:23).

- *For by grace you* [continuously] *have been saved through faith, and that not of yourselves; it is the gift of God* (Ephesians 2:8).

- *In whom the whole building,* [continuously] *being fitted together,* [continuously] *grows into a holy temple in the Lord* (Ephesians 2:21).

- *That we should* [continuously] *no longer* [continuously] *be children,* [continuously] *tossed to and fro and carried about with every wind of doctrine, by the trickery of men, in the cunning craftiness of deceitful plotting, but,* [continuously] *speaking the truth in love, may grow up in all things into Him who* [continuously] *is the head – Christ – from whom the whole body,* [continuously] *joined and* [continuously] *knit together by what every joint supplies, according to the effective working by which every part does its share,* [continuously] *causes growth of the body for the edifying of itself in love* (Ephesians 4:14-16).

- *And do not* [continuously] *be drunk with wine, in which is dissipation; but be* [continuously be being] *filled with the Spirit* (Ephesians 5:18).

- *That He might present her to Himself a glorious church,* [continuously] *not having spot or wrinkle or any such thing, but that she should* [continuously] *be holy and without blemish* (Ephesians 5:27).

- *Therefore, my beloved, as you have always obeyed, not as in my presence only, but now much more in my absence,* [continuously] *work out your own salvation with fear and trembling;* (Philippians 2:12). This passage is addressed to Christians, and so here Paul is clearly referring to "salvation" as an ongoing process (comment is mine).

- *. . . and be found in Him, not* [continuously] *having my own righteousness, which is from the law, but that which is through faith in Christ, the righteousness which is from God by faith; that I may know Him and the power of His resurrection, and the fellowship of His sufferings, being* [continuously] *conformed to His death, if by any means, I may attain to the resurrection from the dead. Not that I have already attained, or am already perfected; but I* [continuously] *press on, that I may lay hold of that for which Christ Jesus has also laid hold of me* (Philippians 3:9-12).

- *Therefore let us, as many as are mature,* [continuously] *have this mind; and if in anything you* [continuously] *think otherwise, God will reveal even this to you* (Philippians 3:15).

- *That you may walk worthy of the Lord, fully pleasing Him, being* [continuously] *fruitful in every good work and* [continuously] *increasing in the knowledge of God* (Colossians 1:10).

- [continuously] *giving thanks to the Father who has qualified us to be partakers of the inheritance of the saints in light. He has delivered us from the power of darkness and conveyed us into the kingdom of the Son of His love. In whom we* [are continuously having] *have redemption through His blood, the forgiveness of sins* (Colossians 1:12-14).

- *And you* [continuously] *are complete in Him, who* [continuously] *is the head of all principality and power* (Colossians 2:10).

- *Let no one* [continuously] *cheat you of your reward,* [continuously] *taking delight in false humility and worship of angels,* [continuously] *intruding into those things which he has not seen,* [continuously] *vainly puffed up by his fleshly mind, and not* [continuously] *holding fast to the Head, from who all the body,* [continuously] *nourished and knit together by joints and ligaments,* [continuously] *grows with the increase that is from God* (Colossians 2:18-19).

- *Do not* [continuously] *lay hands on anyone hastily, nor* [continuously] *share in other people's sins;* [continuously] *keep yourself pure* (1 Timothy 5:22).

- *But you, O man of God,* [continuously] *flee these things and* [continuously] *pursue righteousness, godliness, faith, love, patience, gentleness* (1 Timothy 6:11).

- [Continuously] *Flee also youthful lusts; but* [continuously] *pursue righteousness, faith, love, peace, with those who* [continuously] *call on the Lord out of a pure heart* (2 Timothy 2:22).

- *That the man of God may* [continuously] *be complete, thoroughly equipped for every good work* (2 Timothy 3:17).

- *Who, in the days of His flesh, when He had offered up prayers and supplications, with vehement cries and tears to Him who was able to* [continuously] *save Him from death, and was heard because of His godly fear,* (Hebrews 5:7).

- *Therefore He is also* [continuously] *able to* [continuously] *save to the uttermost those who* [continuously] *come to God through Him, since He always* [continuously] *lives to* [continuously] *make intercession for them* (Hebrews 7:25).

- *For if that first covenant had been faultless, then no place would have been sought for a second. . . "For this is the covenant that I will make with the house of Israel after those days,* [is continuously saying] *says the Lord: I will* [continuously] *put My laws in their mind and* write them on their hearts; *and I will be their God, and they shall be My people. None of them shall teach his neighbor and none his brother, saying 'Know the Lord,' for all shall know Me, from the least of them to the greatest of them. For I will be merciful to their unrighteousness, and their sins and their lawless deeds I will remember no more. "* (Hebrews 8:7, 10).

- *For the law,* [continuously] *having a shadow of the good things* [continually] *to come, and not the very image of the things, can never with these same sacrifices, which they offer continually year by year, make those who* [continuously] *approach perfect* (Hebrews 10:1)

- *By the which will we* [continuously are having been] *sanctified through the offering of the body of Jesus Christ* [once and for all]. *And every priest standeth daily ministering and offering oftentimes the same sacrifices, which can never take away sins; but this man, after he had offered one sacrifice for sins for ever, sat down on the right hand of God; from henceforth expecting till his enemies be made his footstool. For by one offering he hath perfected for ever them* that are [continuously being] *sanctified.* (Hebrews 10:10-14 KJV).

- *"This is the covenant that I will make with them after those days,* [continuously] *says the Lord: I will* [continuously] *put My laws into their hearts, and in their minds I will write them, "* *then He adds, "their sins and lawless deeds I will remember no more. " Now where there is remission of these, there is no longer an offering for sin. Therefore, brethren,* [continuously] *having boldness to enter the Holiest by the blood of Jesus, by a new and* [continuously] *living way which He consecrated for us, through the veil, that* [continuously] *is, His flesh, and having a High Priest over the house of God,* let us [continuously be drawing near] *draw near with a true heart in full assurance of faith, having our hearts sprinkled from an evil conscience and our bodies washed with pure water. Let us* [continuously] *hold fast the confession of our hope without wavering, for he who promised is faithful.* (Hebrews 10:16-23).

- *Make you complete in every good work to do His will,* [continuously] *working in you what is well pleasing in His sight, through Jesus Christ, to whom be glory forever and ever. Amen* (Hebrews 13:21).

- *My brethren, count it all joy when you fall into various trials,* [continuously] *knowing that the testing of your faith* [is continuously producing] *produces patience. But* [continuously be letting] *let patience have its perfect work, that you may be* [continuously] *perfect and complete,*[continuously] *lacking nothing* (James 1:2-4).

- *Of His own will He brought us forth by the word of truth, that we might* [continuously] *be a kind of firstfruits of His creatures* (James 1:18).

- *You* [continuously] *see then that a man is* [continuously] *justified by works, and not by faith only* (James 2:24).

- [Continuously] *Confess your trespasses to one another, and* [continuously] *pray for one another, that you may be healed. The* [continuously] *effective, fervent prayer of a righteous man* [continuously] *avails much* (James 5:16).

- *Who are* [continuously being] *kept by the power of God through faith for salvation ready to be revealed in the last time* (1 Peter 1:5).

- *There is also an antitype which now* [continuously] *saves us – baptism (not the removal of the filth of the flesh, but the answer of a good conscience toward God), through the resurrection of Jesus Christ,* (1 Peter 3:21).

- *Now "If the righteous one is scarcely* [continuously] *saved, where will the ungodly and the sinner appear?"* (1 Peter 4:18).

- *But* [continuously] *grow in the grace and knowledge of our Lord and Savior Jesus Christ. To Him be the glory both now and forever. Amen* (2 Peter 3:18).

- *But if we* [continuously] *walk in the light as He* [continuously] *is in the light, we* [continuously] *have fellowship with one another, and the blood of Jesus Christ His Son* [continuously] *cleanses us from all sin* (1 John 1:7).

- *If we* [continuously] *confess our sins, He* [continuously] *is faithful and just to forgive us our sins and to cleanse us from all unrighteousness* (1 John 1:9).

- *But whoever* [continuously] *keeps His word, truly the love of God is perfected in him. By this we* [continuously] *know that we are in Him* (1 John 2:5).

- *Behold what manner of love the Father has bestowed on us, that we should be called children of God! Therefore the world does not know us, because it did not know Him. Beloved, now we are children of God; and it has not yet been revealed what we shall be, but we know that when He is revealed, we shall be like Him, for we shall see Him as He is. And everyone who has this hope in Him purifies himself, just as He is pure*
(1 John 3:1-3).

"See, you all, what love the Father has given to us, that children of God we may be called; because of this the world is continuously not knowing us, because it did not know Him. Beloved, now, children of God we continuously are, and it has not yet been manifested what we shall be, and we have known that if He may be manifested, <u>like Him we shall be,</u> because we shall see Him as He is. And every one who is continuously having this hope in Him, <u>is continuously purifying himself, even as He is continuously pure.</u> Everyone who is continuously doing the sin also continuously does lawlessness, and the sin continuously is lawlessness [sinning plants "bad roots," and the "bad roots" produce "bad fruit."], and you all have known that He was manifested that our sins He may take away, and sin is continuously not in Him; everyone who is continuously remaining in Him continuously does not sin; and everyone who is continuously sinning has not had personal acquaintance with Him, nor experientially known Him. Little children, let no one continuously lead you all astray; he who is continuously doing righteousness is continuously righteous, <u>even as he is continuously righteous</u> [Don't be deceived. If there is continuously "good fruit," there exists a "good root" (Jesus) in him]" (1 John 3:1-7, <u>My Translation</u> and elaboration).

- *No one has seen God at any time. If we* [continuously] *love one another, God* [continuously] *abides in us, and His love has been perfected in us* (1 John 4:12).

- *Love has been perfected among us in this: that we may* [continuously} *have boldness in the day of judgment; because as He* [continuously] *is, so* [continuously] *are we in this world* (1 John 4:17).

# Section 3

In the passages in this Section, the writers are addressing Christians. Therefore, there is a clear inference that these passages are not referring to the one-time event, which has already happened to them. Thus these passages must be speaking of the ongoing process of sanctification.

- *"But we* [continuously} *believe that through the grace of the Lord Jesus Christ we shall be saved in the same manner as they"* (Acts 15:11).
- *"So now, brethren, I* [continuously] *commend you to God and to the word of His grace, which is* [continuously] *able to build you up and give you an inheritance among all those who are sanctified"* (Acts 20:32).
- *for not the hearers of the law are just in the sight of God, but the doers of the law will be justified* (Romans 2:13).
- *Knowing this, that our old man was crucified with Him, that the body of sin might be done away with, that we should no longer be slaves of sin. For he who has died has been freed* [is justified] *from sin* (Romans 6:6-7).
- *I speak in human terms because of the weakness of your flesh. For just as you presented your members as slaves of uncleanness and of lawlessness leading to more lawlessness, so now present your members as slaves of righteousness for holiness* (Romans 6:19).
- *And do this, knowing the time, that now it is high time to awake out of sleep: for now our salvation is nearer than when we first believed* (Romans 13:11).

- *Now I myself am confident concerning you, my brethren, that you also are* [continuously] *full of goodness, filled with all knowledge,* [continuously] *able also to* [continuously] *admonish one another* (Romans 15:14).
- *But of Him you are in Christ Jesus, who became for us wisdom from God – and righteousness and <u>sanctification</u> and redemption* – (1 Corinthians 1:30).
- *For I know of nothing against myself, yet I am not justified by this; but He who* [continuously] *judges me* [continuously] *is the Lord* (1 Corinthians 4:4).
- *The sting of death is sin; and the strength of sin is the law. But thanks be to God,* [<u>the one continuously giving to us</u>] *<u>victory</u> through our Lord Jesus Christ* (1 Corinthians 15:56-57 KJV).
- *For we are glad when we are weak and you are strong. And this also we pray, that you may be made complete* (2 Corinthians 13:9).
- *Knowing that a man is not* [continuously] *justified by the works of the law but by faith in Jesus Christ, even we have believed in Christ Jesus, that we might be justified by faith in Christ not by the works of the law; for by the works of the law no flesh shall be justified. "But if, while we* [continuously] *seek to be justified by Christ, we ourselves also are found sinners, is Christ therefore a minister of sin? Certainly not!"* (Galatians 2:16-17).
- *For we through the Spirit eagerly wait for the hope of righteousness by faith* (Galatians 5:5)
- *Even when we were* [continuously] *dead in trespasses, made us alive together with Christ (by grace you* [continuously are ones having been] *have been saved)* (Ephesians 2:5).
- *That He would grant you, according to the riches of His glory, to be strengthened with might <u>through His Spirit in the inner man,</u> that <u>Christ may dwell in your hearts through faith</u>; that you, being rooted and grounded in love, may be able to comprehend with all the saints what is the width and length and depth and height – to know the love of Christ which* [is continuously transcending] *passes knowledge; that you may be filled with all the fullness of God* (Ephesians 3:16-19).
- *For the equipping of the saints for the work of ministry, for the edifying of the body of Christ; till we all come to the unity of the*

*faith and of the knowledge of the Son of God, to a perfect man, to the measure of the stature of the fullness of Christ* (Ephesians 4:12-13).

- *That He might sanctify and cleanse her with the washing of water by the word* (Ephesians 5:26).

- *For this reason we also, since the day we heard it,* [continuously] *do not cease to* [continuously] *pray for you, and to* [continuously] *ask that you may be filled with the knowledge of His will in all wisdom and spiritual understanding* (Colossians 1:9).

- *But above all these things put on love, which is the bond of perfection* (Colossians 3:14).

- *Night and day* [continuously] *praying exceedingly that we may see your face and perfect what is lacking in your faith?* (1 Thessalonians 3:10).

- *So that He may establish your hearts blameless in holiness before our God and Father at the coming of our Lord Jesus Christ with all His saints* (1 Thessalonians 3:13).

- *For God did not call us to uncleanness, but to holiness (1 Thessalonians 4:7).*

- *But let us who are of the day be sober, putting on the breastplate of faith and love, and as a helmet the hope of salvation. For God did not appoint us to wrath, but to obtain salvation through our Lord Jesus Christ* (1 Thessalonians 5:8-9).

- [Continuously] *Take heed to yourself and to the doctrine.* [Continuously] *Continue in them, for in* [continuously] *doing this you will save both yourself and those who* [continuously] *hear you* (1 Timothy 4:16).

- *Therefore if anyone cleanses himself from the latter, he will be a vessel for honor, <u>sanctified</u> and useful for the Master, prepared for every good work* (2 Timothy 2:21).

- *For if the blood of bulls and goats and the ashes of a heifer, sprinkling the unclean, sanctifies for the purifying of the flesh, how much more shall the blood of Christ, who through the eternal Spirit offered Himself without spot to God, cleanse your conscience from dead works to* [be continuously serving] *serve the living God?* (Hebrews 9:13-14).

- *Therefore lay aside all filthiness and overflow of wickedness and receive with meekness the implanted word, which is* [continuously] *able to save your souls* (James 1:21).
- *What does it profit, my brethren, if someone* [continuously] *says he has faith but* [continuously] *does not have works?* [Continuously} *Can faith save him?* (James 2:14).
- *Do you* [continuously] *see that faith was working together with his works, and by works faith was made perfect?* (James 2:22).
- *Draw near to God and He will draw near to you. Cleanse your hands, you sinners; and purify your hearts, you double-minded* (James 4:8).
- *And the prayer of faith will save the* [continuously] *sick, and the Lord will raise him up. And if he has* [continuously] *committed sins, he will be forgiven* (James 5:15).
- *Brethren, if anyone among you wanders from the truth, and someone turns him back, let him know that he who turns a sinner from the error of his way will save a soul from death and cover a multitude of sins* (James 5:19-20).
- *But as he who called you is holy, you also be holy in all your conduct* (1 Peter 1:15).
- *As newborn babes, desire the pure milk of the word, that you may grow thereby* (1 Peter 2:2).
- *But <u>sanctify the Lord God in your hearts</u>, and always be ready to give a defense to everyone who* [continuously] *asks you a reason for the hope that is in you, with meekness and fear;* (1 Peter 3:15).
- *But may the God of all grace, who called us to His eternal glory by Christ Jesus, after you have suffered a while, perfect, establish, strengthen, and settle you* (1 Peter 5:10).

# Bibliography

**Brown**, Colin, General Editor (1986). The New International Dictionary of New Testament Theology, 4 Vols. Grand Rapids, MI: Zondervan Publishing House.

**Bultmann,** Rudolf (1960). Existence & Faith. Cleveland, OH: The World Publishing Company.

**Bultmann**, Rudolf (1955). Theology of the New Testament, Parts I-!V. New York, NY: Charles Scribner's Sons.

**Elwell,** Walter A (1984). Evangelical Dictionary of Theology. Grand Rapids, MI: Baker Book House Company.

**Jacobs**, Joan (1976). Feelings. Wheaton, IL: Tyndale House Publishers, Inc.

**Kohn,** Alfie (1980). No Contest. Boston, MA: Houghton Mifflin Company.

**Kurath,** Edward (2010). I Will Give You Rest. Post Falls, ID: Divinely Designed.

**Kurath,** Edward (2012). Exceedingly Great and Precious Promises. Post Falls, ID: Divinely Designed.

**Luther**, Martin, (2003 rpt.). The Bondage Of The Will. Translated by Packer, J.I. and Johnston, O.R. . Grand Rapids, MI: Fleming H. Revell.

**New American Standard Bible.** (1977 rpt). LaHabra, CA: The Lockman Foundation.

**New King James Version of the Holy Bible**. (1983). Nashville, TN: Thomas Nelson Publishers.

**Palmer**, Parker J. (2000). Let your Life Speak. San Francisco, CA: John Wiley & Sons, Inc.

**Siegel**, Daniel J. (1999). The Developing Mind. New York, NY: The Guilford Press.

**Strong**, James LL.D., S.T.D. (1990). The New Strong's Exhaustive Concordance of the Bible. Nashville, TN: Thomas Nelson Publishers.

**Thayer**, Joseph H. D.D. (1977). A Greek-English Lexicon of the New Testament. Grand Rapids, MI: Baker Book House.

**Warren**, Rick. (2002). <u>The Purpose Driven Life</u>. Grand Rapids, MI: Zondervan.

**Wigram**, George V. (1979). <u>The Englishman's Greek Concordance</u>. Grand Rapids, MI: Baker Book House.

**Wuest**, Kenneth S. (1980). <u>The New Testament, An Expanded Translation.</u> Grand Rapids, MI: William B. Eerdmans Publishing Company.

**Young,** Robert. (2005). Modern Young's Literal Translation. Lafayette, IN: Greater Truth Publishers.

**Zodhiates,** Spiros, ThD. (1992). <u>The Complete Wordstudy Dictionary, New Testament.</u> Chattanooga, TN: AMG Publishers.

**Zodhiates**, Spiros, ThD. (1986). <u>The Hebrew-Greek Key Study Bible.</u> Chattanooga, TN: AMG Publishers.

# Resources & Contact Information

## Other Books by Edward Kurath:

- <u>I Will Give You Rest</u>
- <u>I Will Give You Rest Workbook</u>
- <u>I Will Give You Rest Devotional Version</u>
- <u>Exceedingly Great & Precious Promises</u>

## Ways To Buy Books:

- Online: www.divinelydesigned.com

  or

  Online bookstores, such as Amazon.com
- By Phone:  (208) 755-9206
- Mail:  Divinely Designed
  24326 Winder Place
  Golden, Colorado 80403, USA

## Counseling and Seminars

- Online: www. divinelydesigned.com
- E-mail: edkurath @divinelydesigned.com
- Phone:  (208) 755-9206

## Other Resources

In addition to the book, we have other resources available on our website, **www.divinelydesigned.com.**

### Free Information

- Many chapters of books in print
- Chapters of books in audio
- Articles and other resources of interest

### Products For Sale

- All my books in print
- CD's and DVD's of the teachings of "I Will Give You Rest."